The Financial Freedom Blueprint

(A Practical Guide)

By Genyk Lumage

© 2024. Genyk Lumage. All rights reserved.

No part of this book may be reproduced, stored in a retrieval system, or transmitted in any form or by any means, electronic, mechanical, photocopying, recording, or otherwise, without prior written permission of the publisher.

This book is a work of non-fiction. The names, characters, and incidents portrayed in it are a product of the author's knowledge and creativity. Any resemblance to actual events, locales, or persons, living or dead, is entirely coincidental.

Published by Genyk Lumage.
Printed in Printed Worldwide.

Acknowledgments

I would like to express my deepest gratitude to my incredible assistant and inspiration, Enni. Your unwavering support, wisdom, and encouragement have been invaluable throughout the creation of this book. You are a true source of light and strength, and this work would not have been possible without you. Thank you for believing in me and making this journey so extraordinary.

The Financial Freedom Blueprint
(A Practical Guide)
Contents

1. **Introduction** – Page _ _ _ _ _ _ _ _   6
2. **Chapter 1: Financial Flows**
    - *Life is a System* – Page _ _ _ _ _ _ _ _   8
    - *Financial Report* – Page _ _ _ _ _ _ _   14
3. **Chapter 2: The Building of Financial Freedom** – Page _ _ _ _ _ _ _ _ _ _   28
4. **Chapter 3: Manage**
    - *The Purchase Act* – Page _ _ _ _ _ _   37
5. **Chapter 4: Save**
    - *The Savings Program* – Page _ _ _ _ _   48
6. **Chapter 5: Invest**
    - *Freedom Strategy* – Page _ _ _ _ _ _ _   58
    - *Security Plan* – Page _ _ _ _ _ _ _ _ _   72
    - *Protection Plan* – Page _ _ _ _ _ _ _ _   75
    - *Independence Plan* – Page _ _ _ _ _ _ _   79
    - *Freedom Plan* – Page _ _ _ _ _ _ _ _ _   80
7. **Chapter 6: Create** – Page _ _ _ _ _ _ _   83
8. **Chapter 7: Protect**
    - *Protection Strategy* – Page _ _ _ _ _ _ _   110

Hello, dear reader!

This book describes a system of precise actions—"do one-two-three"—that I want to share with you. Let me draw your attention to a VERY IMPORTANT POINT: as you start reading this book, practically from the first page, the emotion of wanting, "I WANT—I REALLY WANT," will automatically transform into "I TAKE ACTION."

Be warned that after reading this book, you will feel a pleasant, tickling sensation of being a free person, empowered by the knowledge you will acquire. However, inaction will constantly remind you of itself through discomfort. Therefore, the decision must be clear: either YES or NO, with no compromises for yourself. If you are not ready to act, it is better to set this book aside for another time.

For those who are firmly determined to improve the financial aspect of their lives and do not want to waste time reading piles of irrelevant material and copied pages from the Internet, this book is for you. In any case, the decision comes from the heart.

This book contains only practical actions with explanations, without unnecessary 'fluff.' By following these actions, you will achieve the desired results in the figures you record in your financial plan.

Money is a tool in our daily lives, and like any tool, it is important to learn how to use it properly. Only then will the results of our lives bring us joy. Without the ability to handle tools, injuries usually occur.

This book will become your 'Key' to simple actions, by performing which you will unlock the backstage door to the mysterious mechanism of the financial system. Financial prosperity does not come from working two or three shifts, but from knowledge turned into actions, ensuring financial growth and security.

There is no need for me to philosophize further. If you have been looking for "What needs to be done to achieve the desired result," then now actions are more important than words!

Prepare to open a new chapter of your life, filled with confidence and financial freedom!

See you on the first page of the first chapter!

Financial Streams

Life is a System

- Everything that is organized and operates daily, year after year, is systematized and forms part of a larger system.

Finance: - is also a system that has its own laws, its own requirements, respect, attention, and protection. It is a deep misconception to think that to invest or start your own business, you need an initial start-up capital. Below you will understand why.

Before you begin building a solid financial foundation, let me show you another system. It is well-known, it is obvious, but it has been structured and positioned in such a way that people discuss it constantly, but only superficially and with dissatisfaction, without ever revealing the true reason.

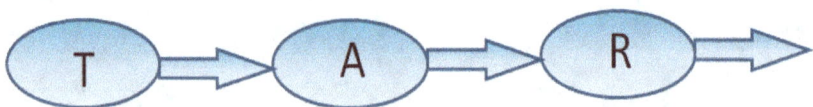

Let's examine the diagram, **where T - Thought; A - Action; R - Result.** How did you end up on this page? Correct, you first had a thought. You knew exactly that somewhere there is a simple system where, by performing clear sequential actions, you achieve the desired result. For this, you specified your question in a search engine and reviewed the suggested pages. Then, showing interest, you performed an action, i.e., purchased the book. As an initial result, this book is now in front of you, and you have started learning. In a month, you will already be able to touch the real, materialized financial *result.*

We will use this universal formula to achieve any desired result, and now we will move on to familiarize ourselves with the basic rule of money.

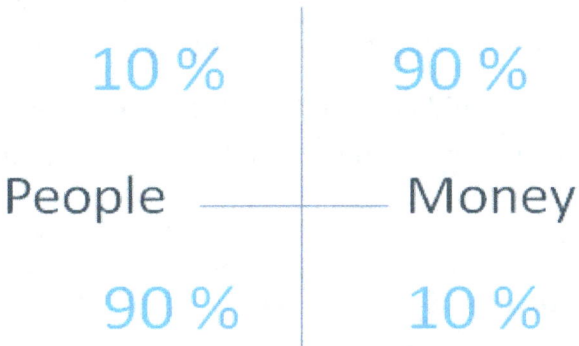

Pay attention to the diagram, on the left side are all people, on the right side is all the money, and the trick is that 10% of people own 90% of all money, and only 10% of the total money is left for 90% of people. I am sure you know this, and you also know that for each of these categories of people, there is one financial problem, which is clearly visible in the diagram;

The first one we hear very often is: - **"Not enough money"**

The second one is: - **"Too much money"**

And what is the problem for most normal people, what do you think? - Correct, ***"not enough money" or "where to get money?"***

And what is the problem for the other category? Correct, ***"where to put it?"*** Agreed, the first arising question might be (is this even a problem?) But here is an example that widely opens your eyes.

Imagine that you have a billion dollars 1,000,000,000, and you are tasked to spend 10,000 dollars every day, without holidays and weekends, before starting your daily activities, i.e., before sitting down to eat, before going to bed, before spending time for pleasure, you first spend and then the whole day is free. Let's count together:

1,000,000,000 \$ ÷ 10,000 \$ = 100,000 days, now look at how many years you would need for such labor:

100,000 ÷ 365 = 273 years 10 months

It turns out that one lifetime is not enough to spend it)))) not even two.

But that's not all, there is a ubiquitous woman named inflation, and she takes a bite of your billion every month, year after year. Let's calculate, if inflation is only 6% per year:

1,000,000,000 × 6% = 60,000,000 $ per year

Now let's look at it monthly:

60,000,000 $ ÷ 12 = 5,000,000 $ per month

And let's consider it daily:

60,000,000 $ ÷ 365 = 164,383 $ per day

And now, how do you feel when you can't solve the problem of "too much money" and lose 164 thousand dollars every day? Mark this as **VERY IMPORTANT**:

"The mindset that creates poverty, when money increases, creates even greater poverty."

And as harsh as it may sound, *POVERTY* is not about the amount of money, poverty is *MINDSET*.

What do you think, what question do those 10% of people who have a lot of money ask? Correct "Where to put the money?"

Let's consider the full picture:

Where to get => Not enough money
Where to put => Too much money

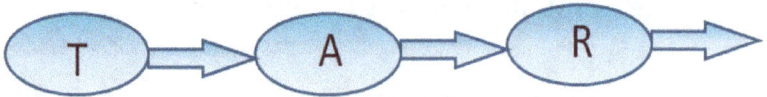

Looking at the diagram, answer this: **"Not enough money"**—is it a thought or a result? Correct, it's a ***result***. And **"Where to get?"**—what is that? Correct, a ***thought***. Let's recall what is primary; this is where the lesson began: correct, **a thought.** So if thought is primary, where will it lead a normal person? That's right, to the result *"not enough money"*, then again to the thought *"where to get"*, and once again to the result *"not enough money."* Remember Robert Kiyosaki's *"Rat Race"*—from birth to the twilight of life, stuck in the same wheel, on the same path, generation after generation.

Here's the discovery of the first secret and your first assignment: constantly air out your mind from the intrusive thought *"where to get money,"* forget entirely about the notion of *"not enough money,"* and always think **"where to put it"**—**where to put a cent, a dollar, or a euro.** Get used to thinking **"where to put it,"** because you always have money. Don't believe me? Open your wallet and look. Now think about where to put it to multiply and save it from inflation. Firmly remember, **"Where to get money and not enough** money" is the mindset of poverty.** This is a habit that must be replaced with its opposite.

Moving to Practice

Take a dollar bill from your wallet, look at it, examine the design, the serial number. You can smell it, taste it, and feel what emotion it evokes in you.

- Agreed, it might be completely insignificant. Now move it to another hand, place it on a shelf, hide it in a book, put it on the table, or the refrigerator. Ask yourself: how exhausted are you from this action? Or, for example, how many universities would you need to graduate from to complete this difficult operation?)))) I can say for sure that you already have all the knowledge, skills, time, and money to perform this action once a day. Let me show you what happens if you start doing this daily and set aside one dollar each day.

Let's calculate: **365 days × 1 $ = 365 $** per year. Easy, right? Over 10 years, this will amount to **3,650 $.** And over 20, 30, 40, 50 years? But here's the twist: using the math of life, not simple school math, if you save **1 $ a day**, in 10 years, you will have **7,174 $.** Notice the difference? Over 20 years, this becomes **29,455 $.** Over 30 years, it grows to **98,657 $.** In 40 years, it becomes **313,587 $.** At 50 years, it's **981,127 $.** And in 60 years, it reaches **3,054,407 $.**

Now you see and understand that the value of a single dollar is entirely different. Of course, no one wants to wait 60 years, but tell me: what do we have at 60 if we live like most normal people? Correct, just a pension, survival, and free tram rides to any part of the world. Now take that dollar again and look at it. What do you see now? A normal person, when holding a dollar, sees only the dollar itself. When a wealthy person holds a dollar, they see *WEALTH*.

A poor person looks at a dollar and does not believe what it can accomplish; in other words, they do not know this. That is why, for them, a dollar is just *"little,"* or *"no money,"* or *"where to get."* A wealthy person knows what wealth a single dollar can create; therefore, they think ***"where to put it."***

Believing is Knowing

According to your faith, it will be given to you, of that we are sure. Believing and knowing are one and the same; therefore, next, we will work on our **faith.**

Financial Report

Look at the diagram: imagine the budget as a balloon. Throughout the month, you inflate it (earnings), and then it deflates (expenses). Then, for another month, you inflate it again (earnings), and once more, it deflates (expenses), leaving it empty.

Most normal people only know this about cash flow, income, and expenses. Hence the question: *"Where to get"* — work more. But there are only 24 hours in a day, which means —*"Not enough money!"*

Remember, **10% of people—THE RICH—know about the existence of two additional sectors in their financial report.** These sectors exist for everyone, but most people do not see or know about them. Here they are:

a. One of the sectors is assets, i.e., what generates income without your involvement.

b. The other is liabilities, i.e., what incurs expenses without your involvement.

On the example of the balloon, this resembles a vacuum cleaner: you connect it to power and press the button. The vacuum cleaner works on its own, sucking air out of the balloon. Do you need to stand next to it? Look at these examples:

You went on vacation for a month, came back, reached into your mailbox, and found a notice:

"You were absent for a month, did not use electricity, water, garbage disposal, the elevator, or walked on the stairs, nor did you bring dust into the entrance. Thank you for everything. The total utility bill is ***ZERO!***)))" Correct? I think I may have made a small mistake about the zero. This means the house is a liability, and it doesn't matter whether you're at home or not—it always incurs **expenses.**

An example with a car: You know it needs to be fueled and maintained. Sure, you can consider a taxi, which generates income. But the car doesn't drive around the city by itself; it needs to be driven. This requires time, making it a liability.

But these examples can be reconsidered differently. You could rent out the apartment under favorable conditions. Then, after a month, it would pay for utilities and generate income. Similarly, negotiate with a car rental service, where fuel is the renter's responsibility, repairs are on their account, and you receive daily rental income. Now, your liability turns into an **asset** (in the first case, it incurred expenses without your involvement; in the second, it generates income without your involvement).

These are examples. It doesn't mean you need to rent everything out tomorrow and move into a cave :-).

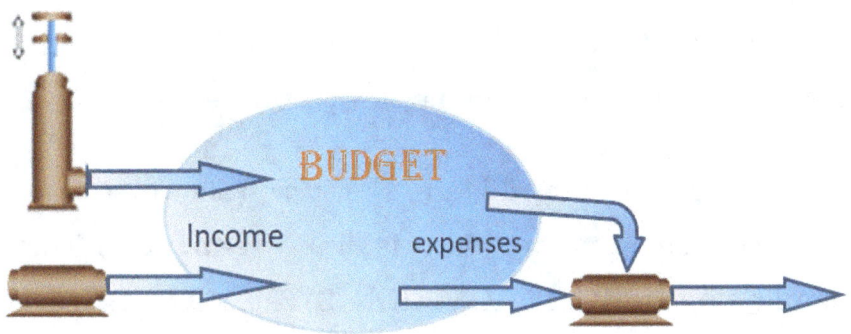

Now let's consider all of this in a holistic and broader way. The final arrow in expenses means that money doesn't disappear into the air; it moves from your pocket to someone else's. Money doesn't vanish; it transitions from one person to another. If you spent one dollar today, at that very moment, someone else earned it. If you lost a thousand dollars at the market, someone else found it there, at the same place. If you deposited money in the bank and it disappeared there, it didn't actually vanish—it went into someone else's pocket. Thus, what is an expense for you is income for someone else. But that's not all: "What is *a liability* for you, is *an asset* for someone else. The same thing can be both an *asset* and a *liability*, depending on how you use it." Remember how 10% of people think? Correct:

"Where to put it". Here's your first answer: **"INTO AN ASSET"**. We will study and examine assets further.

The very first and most IMPORTANT ASSET is **THINKING**. Poverty in thinking is a destructive liability. Poverty, from the word *poor*, truly leads to destruction when money lands in the hands of a poor person. Big money brings big destruction.

POVERTY is the most terrible sin. There is no sin worse than poverty. The root cause of poverty is simply **ignorance**. This means developing HOLISTIC VISION, SYSTEMIC THINKING, and mastering FINANCIAL LITERACY. That's exactly what you are doing right now. You've already invested in it. That's why you're here. Congratulations, and let's move on to the topic:

Financial Flows

Let's examine the flow of the **"Poor Class"**. Pay attention to the diagrams.

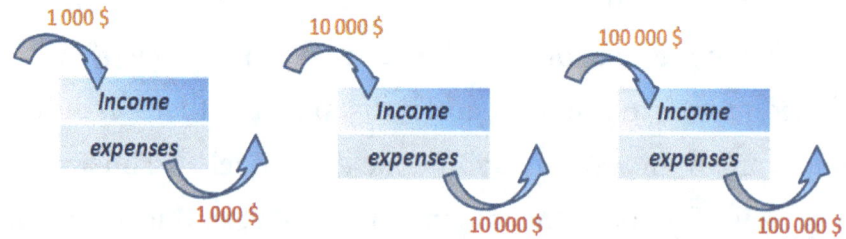

Take note of *"The poor only spend"*. What comes in also goes out. Looking at the first diagram: one thousand came in, and one thousand went out. What type of flow is this? —

Correct, the flow of the *poor class*. On the second diagram, 10,000 $ came in, and 10,000 $ went out. What type of flow is this? — Right, it's also the **poor's flow**. Now, look at the third diagram: 100,000 $ came in, and 100,000 $ went out. What class is this? — Exactly, it's the flow of a poor person with a high salary. They are neither financially free nor wealthy. Just think: if tomorrow this flow stops, and everything has always gone out, but they've already become accustomed to such income, how would they feel? What difference does it make how much they earn if, by the end of the month, the balloon is always empty, and they need to wake up again in the morning to pump their pump? After all, the liabilities bought with such amounts demand their due.

Now see, "normal" people think that if the income is a million, it means the person is wealthy. But wealthy people KNOW for certain: if everything that comes in always goes out, it's POVERTY, regardless of income. And it's the financial report that doesn't let them deceive themselves.

But this isn't the scariest flow. There's an even scarier one, where the faster you run, the faster you need to run. True rat races (remember Robert Kiyosaki's book "Rich Dad, Poor Dad"). It can't get worse—this is the flow of the **middle class.** Let's consider the example of **"Here's what: - He got lucky"**.

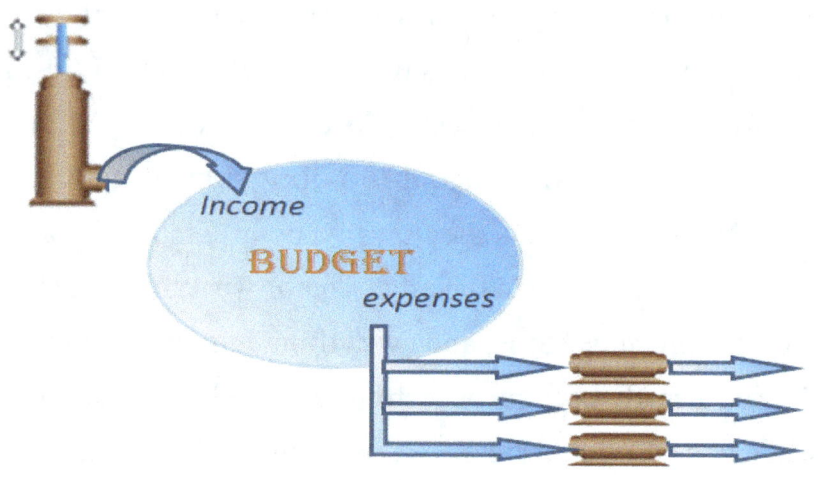

- There was a **normal** person, pumping their balloon at the beginning of the month, earning 2,000 $. Deflated it and pumped again. And then Lady Luck came visiting: they won a jackpot in the lottery—3,000,000 $. And their small apartment suddenly felt tight; of course, they needed to expand. But in the new house, everything is old: the wallpaper doesn't match their taste, and they need new furniture. Public transportation became uncomfortable, and, naturally, a millionaire can't ride buses. They need a car, preferably a top-tier one. Suddenly, their soul started yearning for travel: to see the world and show themselves off.

Friends remembered them, respected them, even those who used to make sand pies in kindergarten. They need to celebrate with expensive gifts. Relatives will surely show up before they even get back from the bank, asking for loans. If they refuse, the relatives will feel offended. And how soon do you think they'll run out of money? Much faster than they could imagine. And here's the kicker: a third of this amount, about 1,000,000 $.—they won't even recall where it went.

And what do they start doing now? Correct: going back to their pump to inflate the balloon. But now, there's a twist: the pump only gives 2,000 $. And they bought liabilities worth 4,000 $. monthly expenses. They still need to eat, and their clothes wear out. But they now have a habit of living on a different amount. So what's their problem now: *Too much money or not enough?* What's the question they keep asking? **"Where to get more"**. Because our minds are so inventive, "normal" people will always find a "normal" answer. They'll find someone to lend them money—credits or another job. Debt doesn't solve the problem; it's an additional liability, another vacuum. Our **"lucky winner"** has no idea how this system works and doesn't even suspect that if they increase their income, expenses will also grow. And now they work two jobs; their income is catching up to their expenses. Caught up. But now expenses have grown to 5,500 $ instead of 4,000 $. Why? First, taxes: higher income means higher taxes. Second, debts: debts grow, and so do interest rates. Third, liabilities: remember how they work? Liabilities grow on their own year by year, taking more money. Now their expenses exceed their income. So, what's their problem? **"Not enough money"**. And what question do they keep asking again and again? Who do you think wins in this system? And stopping isn't an option; they can only accelerate and run faster and faster in circles. This is what we call *"rat races"*. The book *"Rich Dad, Poor Dad"* explains this very well in detail. Many talented and smart people end up in this rat circle for one simple reason: ***"Financial ignorance."***

The middle class flow is characterized by ***"buying liabilities, thinking they are assets."***

Never forget: the same thing can be either an asset or a liability. It depends on how you use it. Look: even debt (credit). Take 10,000,000 $ for a year at 10% interest and invest it at 20%. After a year, you have 1,000,000 $.

Take 10,000,000 at 10% — expenses: 1,000,000

Invest 10,000,000 at 20% — income: 2,000,000

Profit: **1,000,000 $**

Now, tell me, what question arose in your mind just now? ***"Where to invest"*** (put). Correct, so the result is real. I omit the question ***"where to get"*** because it's unnecessary and irrelevant; as soon as you find where to invest, the question of "where to get" will disappear by itself. Very few people can answer the question of "where to invest." And you'll have people asking to invest with you but without the knowledge of where to put it.

The third flow is: - **"The Flow of the Rich"**

Take note: **"RICH PEOPLE BUY ASSETS."**

So let's start creating our ***"financial plan."***

Write down the first point (the first secret): **"Pay yourself first!"**

Everyone has some kind of regular income. It's different for everyone, but it's always there!!!

"YOURSELF" first, because when you spend money, someone else gets it: the one you pay—the seller, the banker, some stranger. But which sector should part of your expenses go to so that YOU get the income? Correct, the **"assets"** sector. But typically, *"normal"* people don't do this, they don't know, they don't see the first word—***FIRST.*** From every ***"regular income" 10% pay yourself***, save it not as a stash but in a designated box to later invest in an asset (this will be explained in detail below). I understand that you might think you barely make enough, so how can you save? But analyze this: if you're short 100 $ to make a purchase, I guarantee that 90 $ won't suffice either. And digging deeper, you'll see that from purchases made for 1,000 $ in a month, one hundred dollars certainly went towards trinkets that have already been forgotten for lack of use. But when you start paying yourself and buying assets, you have a chance to break free from the rat race. And here's a very **IMPORTANT** point: pay yourself first, then spend the rest. No "I'll save after shopping" or other fantasies. Save for yourself first and forget about it. If your hand reaches in to take it because you really need it, Bite your hand right away)))))!!!

We're done with the habits of the *"poor"*.

Let's briefly examine the mechanism that must not be overlooked, as it sharpens focus. Look at why it is necessary to pay yourself and create your own personal assets. First and foremost, we form our financial freedom and financial security—this is clear. Until this is done, any employee is the most reliable asset for the owner. The worker comes and works, takes care of themselves, feeds themselves, dresses themselves. When the owner pays them, it is essentially a monthly investment in an asset; the owner invests one amount per month, triples it or more the next month, reinvests it, and multiplies it again. Thus, all workers are the best assets. But this mechanism must be viewed more broadly. The government of any country deliberately invests billions in raising and educating our children, i.e., in their future assets. From a young age, habits are cultivated: getting up early, going somewhere, listening to educational programs all day, and returning home in the evening. Notice that by the 6th grade, a child already knows they will work—not **"LIVE,"** but *"work"*—whether in the poor class or the middle class, they will work for 35 years straight. That's an asset, isn't it? But that's not all. The salary given to an employee as an investment in an asset also needs to be reclaimed, and in such a way that the worker gladly gives it up. This is where TV commercials and well-organized stores come into play. Notice how everything in a store is meticulously arranged on shelves, looking tempting. This is intentionally designed so that when you enter, you leave with an empty wallet, without being explicitly persuaded to buy anything. It turns out that money is invested in a worker as an asset, bringing significant profits over 35 years. Then, the money given monthly (to support the asset) is taken back through stores—everything! Ask yourself how often you go to a store for one thing but end up buying either something unnecessary or far more than planned? Therefore, **pay yourself first,** because every cent of yours is being hunted, and if you don't save it, someone will take it from you. It is necessary to both spend and create **assets** until the cash flow from assets reaches the level of *financial freedom.* Look at the diagram to see how cash flow looks then. Note that you no longer need to pump the pump; it's time to make your dreams come true.

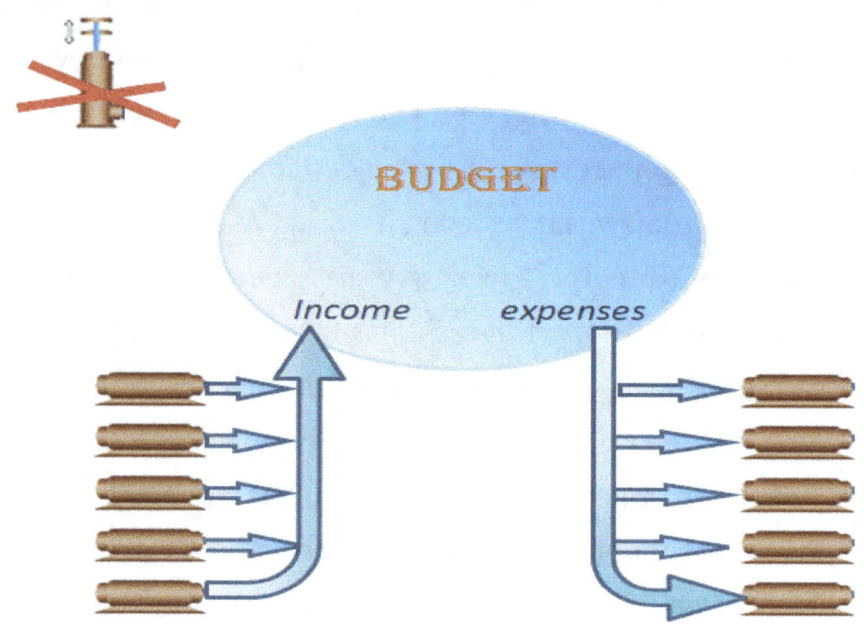

 You are a financially free person! Looking at your financial plan, you know you can buy a beautiful house and an expensive car. Who says that's bad? Who says traveling is bad? Who says LIABILITIES are bad? They are harmful when they RUIN LIFE, but if they help strengthen **HEALTH**, enrich life with **EMOTIONS**, bring us together, strengthen our **RELATIONSHIPS**, and allow us to enjoy **FREEDOM**, then they are wonderful. And if they help us **DISCOVER OURSELVES** as *WEALTHY PEOPLE,* who would dare to say that's bad?!

Now you can take a heavier hammer, approach your pump, and do with it what you've always dreamed of; now you have compressors that continuously pump finances for you.

What do you think a schoolchild, who hasn't yet become *"normal"* and knows how to dream, wants to be when they grow up—poor, middle-class, or rich?

If rich, whom do they look up to first? And what do they see? Only what is visible. When they grow up, they start buying liabilities, spending money, taking loans, and accelerating in the rat race.

Let's wrap up this topic and summarize the material covered:

1. Poverty is not the absence of money but a ***state of mind;***
2. Poverty thinks, **"Where to get money?"** Wealth thinks, **"Where to invest?"**
3. The more money poverty has, **the greater the poverty;**
4. Wealth equals: **Me + financial report;**
5. What is an expense for one is **income for another;**
6. What is a liability for one is **an asset for another;**
7. There are three cash flows: **"poor," "middle-class," and "rich;"**
8. The poor **only spend;**
9. The middle class buys **liabilities;**
10. The rich buy **assets.**

Now let's explore the connecting chain and move on to building our financial freedom structure.

What do you think is the purpose of a human being?

Their purpose is to **"BE HAPPY."**

And what is the purpose of money?

 - **"To SERVE HUMANITY,"** meaning the direct purpose of money is:

 - **To serve humans so they can be happy!**

We have seen the monetary system through the prism of the FINANCIAL REPORT MODEL. Now it is easy for us to understand how the monetary system works, what elements make up the system, which cash flows lead to financial freedom, and which lead to dependence on money. Now let us consider HOW EXACTLY to use the knowledge gained to make money SERVE us.

Building Financial Freedom

Respect

To better understand how money works, in the previous topic we used the FINANCIAL REPORT MODEL. Such a model helps to see how the financial system is STRUCTURED and how it WORKS. To understand how to CREATE cash flows (assets) that lead to financial freedom, we will use another model, a model of the financial system called the ***"BUILDING OF FINANCIAL FREEDOM."***

Let's imagine money as living entities that are meant to serve us and that, like us, need care and respect. Imagine that money goes where it feels best, where it is cared for, where conditions are created for it, and it settles in such a comfortable house. And we put up a sign *"A House Where Money Lives."*

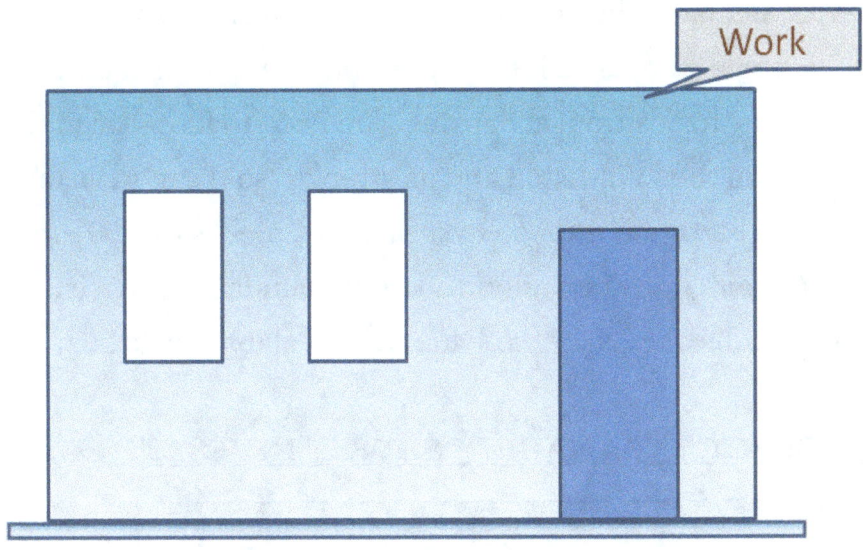

The walls of the house represent **"CREATE."**

But for most people, who build a house for money consisting only of walls, it often sounds like *"Work."*

Tell me, would you live in a house with just walls?

Money is no different. It doesn't want to live in a house without a roof. What if there's "financial bad weather" in the country? Rain, for example, or hail. What would it do then? What would you do?
 But let's imagine a good outcome, and somehow you managed to keep money in such a "house." You continue to earn more and more. Your walls grow higher and higher. There's even more money—the walls grow even taller. What do you think will happen if the walls keep growing but there's no foundation?

Correct, it will collapse during any bad weather—and on whom? Correct again, on the one building those walls. I'm sure you know people who had a lot of money but are now in debt. To prevent the house from collapsing, you need to first design the house, plan the foundation and its strength so it can withstand "financial earthquakes"—so to speak. This means the ***"House for Money"*** must be built on a strong foundation, consisting of several slabs. Each of these foundation slabs has its own name:

"RESPECT," "MANAGE," "SAVE," "INVEST."

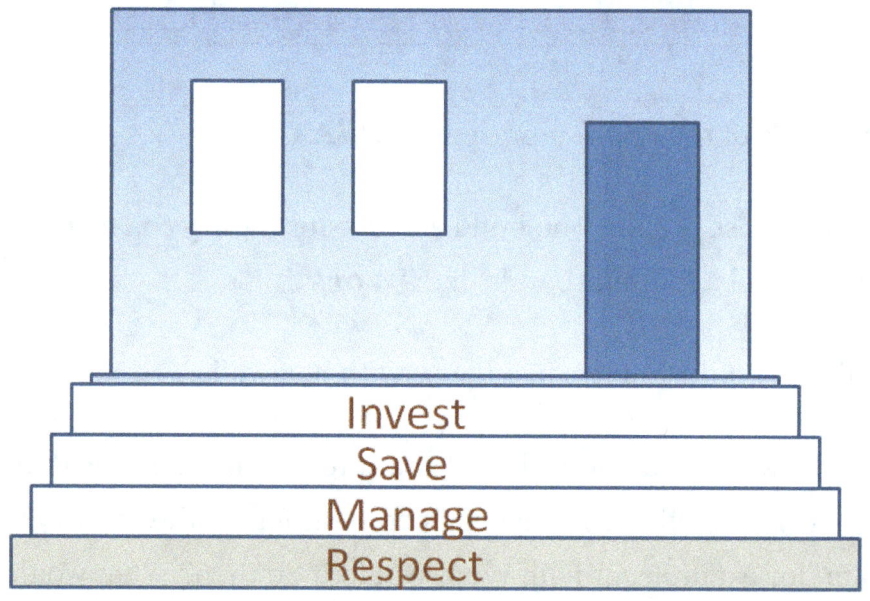

You've probably heard that money needs to be **RESPECTED**, but do you think this is something you learn, or is it enough to tell the portrait of the man on the bill "I respect you"? Don't you think the main foundation slab will come to you as enlightenment, and there's no need to learn it? Now we will need some knowledge of math—not school math, but math you'll enjoy. To do this, we'll consider a real example. Let's say you can afford to set aside $300 per month for your future, and to keep it out of sight, you take it to the bank and deposit it in an account at 3% annual interest (higher rates exist, but let's stick with the central bank). The bank uses your money throughout the year and at the end of the term, returns your $300 plus $9 in interest. Does this math make sense? $300 × 3% = $9.

But now you're financially savvy, and you deposit your money at 3% annual interest, but not simple interest—compound interest. Let me explain with an example. Suppose you come to the bank and agree to deposit $300 monthly into your account, but the bank will pay you 3% not once a year, but 0.25% monthly: 3% annually / 12 months = 0.25% monthly. Under these terms, at the end of the month, the bank will credit you with 0.25% = $0.75. On the first day of the next month, you bring another $300 to the bank, but before depositing it, you withdraw your honestly earned $0.75 for the month and then make your next monthly deposit of $300.75, including the interest earned for the month. Now your deposit account balance is not $600 but $600.75. Is this math clear?

$300 + $0.75 interest + $300 = $600.75.

The second month passes, and the bank credits you with 0.25% again, but now not on $600 but on the entire $600.75, which amounts to $1.5 in interest. On the first day of the third month, you repeat the same operation: bring your $300 deposit, withdraw $1.5 earned over the month, add it to the $300 monthly deposit, and place $302.25 in your account. Thus, your deposit account balance will no longer be $900 but $902.25. Does this math make sense?

$600.75 + $1.5 interest + $300 = $902.25.

I won't describe each month in detail. Let's look at a table showing the result after a year of setting aside just $300 per month.

Month	Start	Interest	Attachments	End
1	300.00	0.75	300.00	600.75
2	600.75	1.50	300.00	902.25
3	902.25	2.26	300.00	1 204.51
4	1 204.51	3.01	300.00	1 507.52
5	1 507.52	3.77	300.00	1 811.29
6	1 811.29	4.53	300.00	2 115.82
7	2 115.82	5.29	300.00	2 421.11
8	2 421.11	6.05	300.00	2 727.16
9	2 727.16	6.82	300.00	3 033.98
10	3 033.98	7.58	300.00	3 341.56
11	3 341.56	8.35	300.00	3 649.91
12	3 649.91	9.12	300.00	3 959.03

The interest totaled: **59.03 $**

So, over the year, you saved 3,659.03 $. Of this amount, 59.03 $ is interest, and 3,600 $ is your money. I won't detail the second, third, etc., years. Take a calculator and calculate it yourself. This is easy and very useful for practice, as it will help you create and continuously adjust your financial plan. For now, I'll show you the numbers 10 years ahead, saving just 300 $ monthly.

Years	Investment	Interest	Accumulation
1	3 600	49,91	3 649.91
2	7 200	210,84	7 410.84
3	10 800	486,15	11 286.15
4	14 400	879,34	15 279.34
5	18 000	1 393,98	19 393.98
6	21 600	2 033,79	23 633.79
7	25 200	2 802,54	28 002.54
8	28 800	3 704,18	32 504.18
9	32 400	4 742,75	37 142.75
10	36 000	5 922,4	41 922.40

In 10 years, your total savings will be **41,922.4 $**. Personal contributions: 36,000 $. Interest: 5,922.4 $. Now let's continue saving 300 $ monthly for another 10 years and see what we get.

Years	Investment	Interest	Accumulation
11	39 600	7 247,43	46 847.43
12	43 200	8 722,24	51 922.24
13	46 800	10 351,42	57 151.42
14	50 400	12 139,65	62 539.65
15	54 000	14 094,78	68 091.78
16	57 600	16 212,79	73 812.79
17	61 200	18 507,80	79 707.80
18	64 800	20 982,10	85 782.10
19	68 400	23 641,16	92 041.16
20	72 000	26 490,59	98 490.59

In 20 years, your total savings will be **98,490.59 $**. Of this, personal contributions: **72,000 $**, and interest: **26,490.59 $**. At this point, your total savings of 98,490.59 $ will provide you with a monthly income of 246 $. This is the simplest way to accumulate savings since, on average, everyone works for 30–35 years in their life. I understand that not everyone has the time to wait that long))) and the interest rate is very small. Therefore, how to accelerate this process, reduce risks, and choose the right banks will be discussed later.

But take into account that this action is very **IMPORTANT and one of the basics for creating your financial**

freedom and forming financial habits.

Now let's consider financial investments with capitalization (compound interest) at 18% annually for 10 years.

Years	Investment	Interest	Accumulation
1	3 600	371	3 971
2	7 200	1 519	8 719
3	10 800	3 596	14 396
4	14 400	6 783	21 183
5	18 000	11 297	29 297
6	21 600	17 400	39 000
7	25 200	25 400	50 600
8	28 800	35 669	64 469
9	32 400	48 651	81 051
10	36 000	64 651	100 877

In 10 years, your total savings will be **100,877 $**, providing you with a monthly income of **1,513 $**.

And in 20 years, performing the same actions, your total savings will amount to **703,046 $**. Of this, personal contributions: **72,000 $**, and interest: **631,046 $**. Now, your total savings of **703,046 $** will provide you with a monthly income of **10,545**
I want to immediately address the question: "What if the bank collapses?" Or perhaps an even more colorful picture with exquisite horrors about what could happen to money that hasn't even reached the bank yet.)))) Further details will explain how to minimize risks by 99.9%. But I can confidently say that if you save 0 $ monthly for your future, then with a 100% guarantee,

in a month, a year, 10 years, etc., until retirement, your accumulated amount will equal zero and will provide a monthly income of zero.)))) My goal is not to impose actions that bring discomfort. I am showing possibilities, and the decision is yours alone, only yours!!!))))

* Moving to the next section, let me give an example *:-
"Investment" Your financial resources are like parents deciding what kind of life they want to live: enjoying life alone or giving the world children. If they decide to create a family, the interest is their children, and compound interest is their grandchildren. The sooner you start investing, the faster your "family" grows. For example, with capital investment under compound interest, your grandchildren appear as early as the third month.

Now imagine: You dream of a large family with children, grandchildren, and even great-grandchildren. What kind of house would you build for them? Without a foundation, missing one wall, or without a roof? Of course not! You want the house to be sturdy, with space for every member of your "financial family."

Your foundation is regular investing.
Your walls are smart strategies that preserve your capital.
Your roof is the protection of your assets, ensuring that no storms destroy your family.

Manage

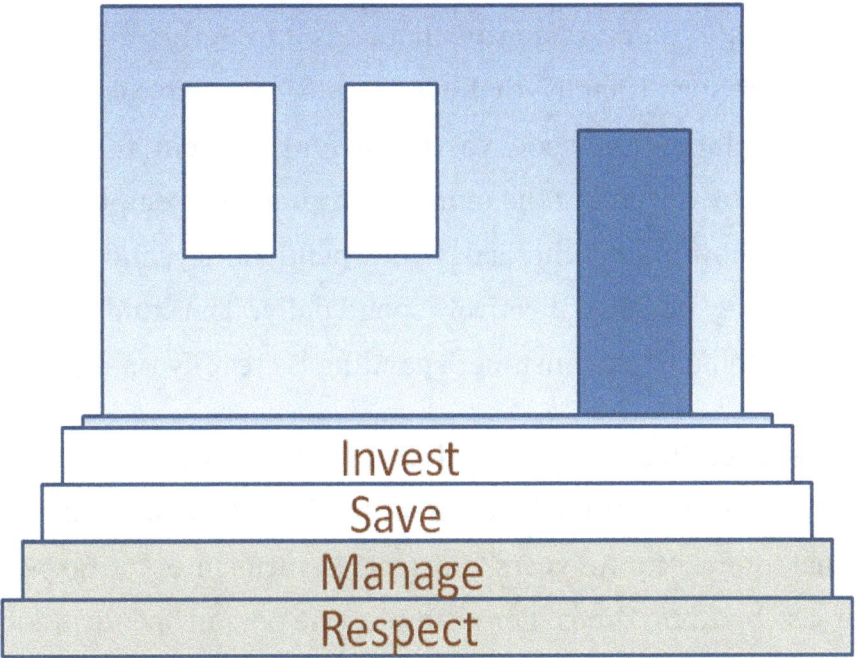

Now we move on to the next foundational slab of our financial house—**"MANAGE."**

We receive money, and how do we spend it? There are three possible answers:

1. We **spend** it.
2. We **invest** it.
3. We **donate** it.

What do you think most of us spend the majority of our money on? Correct—food, clothing, utilities; in other words, spending. And let's remember, what are our expenses? That's right, our *expenses* are someone else's *income*. You feel hungry on the street, it's far from home, so you stop at a café, treat yourself, and leave $20 there. Instantly, that adds $20 to the café owner's financial report. Imagine that over a month you have coffee here, buy clothes and shoes there, pay for beer, rent, fuel, go on vacation—by the end of the month, your budget is empty.))) Calculate how many times a day you spend money, and how much money do WE collectively spend daily? The stubborn statistics tell us that consumer spending is steadily rising.

Now let's recall: by how much does $1 grow if we don't spend it but invest it in a mutual investment fund at 18% compound annual interest for 40 years? Correct, $1 turns into $1,269.7—an increase by 1,269 times. For example, one person spends $208 a month at a store. That money then goes to another business owner, then another, and eventually, the money reaches a financially literate individual who invests it in the same mutual investment fund at 18% compound annual income and doesn't touch it. Over 40 years, this money grows to $264,097.09. Now multiply this amount by the country's population; for easy calculations, let's assume 50,000,000 people:

$208 × 50,000,000 = $10,400,000,000.

Now you truly understand what an asset a country's population is to those who use this money for investment purposes.

Have you calculated how many times an average person makes purchases daily? And how much time have we spent learning

HOW TO BUY? The simple answer: "ALL OUR LIVES," because we buy every day.))) And here's the irony: buying doesn't mean we've learned how to buy. It's like a mischievous student who goes to school to hang out but says, "I'm studying at school."

Let's recall how a teacher enters the classroom: "Good morning, children. Today and henceforth, I will be teaching you the most interesting subject. We will study something you will do daily throughout your adult life—on average, five times a day. We'll study something you already love doing. So, children, write down today's lesson topic: **'HOW TO SPEND MONEY WISELY.'** How many times and for how many seconds did we study this topic in school?"

Look what happens: supermarket employees are trained daily on how to serve customers. Sales managers attend monthly trainings, and directors of large stores regularly go to specialized seminars on the art of selling. Researchers study us thoroughly, day and night; entire institutions work on this. They know everything about us—our motives for purchases, what and why we buy. They analyze it all and then teach it to sellers. And what do sellers learn? To sell, sell, sell—day after day, month after month, year after year, decade after decade. And then we walk into the supermarket with a smile, all dressed in white. How many seconds were we taught in school the art of **BUYING?** That's why, if we do something daily, several times a day, month after month, year after year, we need to become professionals at it.

You surely know how most "normal" people shop. To see it, just recall or observe in a supermarket. Let me show you how a "not normal" but wealthy minority spends money.

ACT OF PURCHASING

1. **Engage REASON;**
2. **Create a LIST;**
3. **Get a DISCOUNT;**
4. **Pay LATER;**
5. **Buy in BULK;**
6. **Be a REGULAR CLIENT;**
7. **DOCUMENT the purchase.**

- The act of shopping can look very different! Imagine a person enters a supermarket without any knowledge of financial savings schemes (without financial literacy). With $1.5, they can probably buy the cheapest ice cream, and they just happen to have $1.5 in their pocket. They gaze at the ice cream, enchanted by its appealing packaging. It's hot outside, there's pleasant music playing, and a charming voice whispers just to them: *"Tastes just like childhood."* Saliva starts flowing as they reminisce about how delicious ice cream was in their childhood, right?))) And suddenly, the little dragon inside wakes up. You know, there's one in each of us, installed since childhood, called

"BUY SOMETHING USELESS."))) As soon as this little dragon opens its eyes, it starts shouting: "Buy it! You absolutely must buy it! You deserve it! You've worked hard, you've got money, you've earned this! Why be stingy? You only live once!" The person originally came for a toothbrush, but they are, after all, a normal person. What do they see? In one hand, $1.5—just a piece of paper. It's not much; they can always earn more. But when they look at the ice cream, WOW! So refreshing, so creamy, and the dragon tugs at their sleeve, whining: "Buy it! You remember how much you wanted ice cream?" Of course, those $1.5 end up in the pocket of the supermarket owner, exchanged for melting ice cream dripping down their hands.

Now let's look at the act of shopping from the perspective of someone financially literate. They enter the same supermarket, with the same music playing, the same ice cream on display, the same heat outside, and the same sweet voice saying: "Tastes just like childhood." But what does this person see? Remember when we calculated how much $1 could grow in 40 years at 18% annual compound interest? That's right—it grows 1,269.7 times. And this person sees in one hand "WOW," but in the other hand, they don't see $1.5; they see $1,903.85 (a BIG WOW). This is why they've become wealthy—because they've rid themselves of "normality," and the little dragon can't influence them. But that doesn't mean that from now on, treats and food are a thing of the past.))) Not at all—let's look at point **2** in our act of shopping.

CREATE A LIST: A shopping list is created not in the store, staring at the ice cream, but at home. In the store, this person looks at their shopping list, sees no ice cream on it, calmly moves on, and buys everything on the list. Why make the list at home? Because at home, you're on your own turf, without flashing screens showing constant ads or sweet, mesmerizing voices tempting you to buy unnecessary items. At home, you know exactly what you need today, tomorrow, for the week, and so on. But in the store, you're on foreign territory—the very place where they watch you and actively hunt for your money. Without your shopping list, their hunt will be 100% successful because they know exactly what they want and invest heavily to achieve it.

You've probably seen families shopping in supermarkets. The man, holding a pouch, pushes the cart while grumbling on his phone. The woman flutters around, wanting to buy half the store because everything smells so good, shines so brightly, and looks so appealing—famous brands, logos, soft music, mesmerizing voices. Their eyes wander everywhere, and the little dragon inside yells: "Buy some junk! Buy it! Just buy it already!" She turns to him plaintively: "Look at this sweater. Let's get it?" He replies: "Fine, just hurry; we don't have time." And package after package of oh-so-necessary things flies into the cart. At checkout, he looks at the overflowing cart of absolute essentials, pulls out a wad of cash, licks his fingers, and begins feeding the pockets of the store owner while emptying his own. From the register, a long receipt slithers out, filled with numbers and ending with a cheerful note: "Thank you for shopping."

Now, let's see how a financially literate shopper behaves in the same store. They grab a cart, pull out their list, and carefully place only listed items into the cart. Suddenly, they notice an item they forgot to include in their list. Have you ever shopped with a list? It happens, right? What does this shopper do? Correct—they keep shopping according to their list, check out at the register, go home, and then add that forgotten item to their list for the next shopping trip.))))) Crazy, right?)))

This practice can be very satisfying in action. When I started, I slightly modified this shopping rule for myself. I decided that if I saw a genuinely necessary item I forgot to include in my list, I'd add it to the list of next purchases when I got home. An interesting fact that I knew but wasn't fully prepared for: after leaving the store, the item often seemed completely unnecessary—or even forgotten by the time I reached checkout. This is the power of being on foreign territory, the effects of advertising, and other traps set for shoppers. This is why the first two steps, **"Engage Reason" and "Create a List,"** should always be done on your own turf—at home.

What does it mean to create a list? It's simple: sit down and write out everything you need to buy for the next day, week, month, or year. You can always adjust and compile the list on your own turf—at home. And what does it mean to **engage reason?** Let's break it down.

The Mind — It's short-sighted. To the mind, only what's visible to the eyes is real. And so, "wants" are instantly triggered in the here and now: the eyes see, the dragon wakes up, and starts tugging at your sleeve, pulling out your "want." As soon as it pulls it out, you buy the most essential unnecessary thing in the world.

Reason — It sees beyond the present moment. To reason, what's real includes not just what is, but also what was and what will be. This is why, before going shopping, you need to switch off the mind, remember the value of a dollar, and stick to buying only what's on your list. Make it your golden rule: all purchases must be made from the list. Without a list, the dragon wakes up and disables both **mind and reason** in exchange for large bags of "wants." At home, with an empty wallet, unloading those bags, you marvel: "I went out for a toothbrush, and look at all this!"

Here's the takeaway:

Having a **"Shopping List"** — *This is our dream.*

No **"Shopping List"** — *This is someone else's dream.*

How does an average person shop? - *They don't buy—and regret it. They buy—and regret it too!*

How does a wealthy person shop? - **They don't buy—and are happy. They buy—and are three times happier.**

Would you like to know how to become financially independent, even if you don't have a single free dollar to save? One word, just one word, and if you use it correctly, you'll always have enough money each month to save and invest.
 - That word is **"DISCOUNT!**
 Do you know what a $1 discount every day means? - It's $30 a month, and in 35 years, this amounts to $1,052,925, which provides a monthly income of $12,635 at a percentage rate. Agree, this is already a decent pension nowadays. Of course, not all of us have that much time ahead. How to speed up this process, I will describe below, but for now, the essence is clear, and you understand what a discount means. Don't hesitate to always ask for a discount—it's a game. Just start playing the discount game, and you'll see that they will begin giving it to you, even if you're not buying anything!))) Getting a discount is the same as earning money. Now let's calculate: with good supermarket purchases, saying the word "discount" three times can earn you $150 or more. And to earn this same amount at work, you'd need to work 3 hours or more. Here's the result of the magical word - **DISCOUNT**, and this word alone is enough to make you a financially free person. And here's the only reason we don't get discounts—*when we don't ask for them!*

Mark for yourself the **MOST IMPORTANT AND BIGGEST SECRET** of poor people: This secret is so great that they don't even realize it: - The favorite prices of poor people are *retail*. Yes, they talk about buying cheaper, but they buy everything more expensively, i.e., retail, and they don't even realize it because those are their favorite prices!

When you get home and make a shopping list, ask yourself: is it possible that what I'm buying retail could be purchased wholesale? Just ask yourself this and don't rush to answer. Familiar scenario? On the way home from work, you drop by the store, buy some random items for dinner, and a couple of eggs for breakfast; the fridge is constantly empty. Now look at point five **"BUY WHOLESALE."**

The mechanism of this system, I started applying while in Poland. Back then, I firmly decided: for one month, I would do everything exactly according to the points I composed. The final result would show me its effectiveness.))) In Poland, practically all stores are supermarkets, and I simply started buying according to my list, wholesale for the week. That is, I only went grocery shopping once a week. Imagine my surprise at the end of the month when, in my accounting program under "expenses," they were reduced by 150 zlotys ($51). And this despite the fact that store prices hadn't changed—just the approach to shopping. Moreover, the fridge was never empty. The system, of course, worked 100%, and starting from the next month, I began shopping at the supermarket every two weeks, buying even more in bulk when possible. Expenses decreased by another 55 zlotys ($18.3), even though the grocery list remained unchanged. If there was a promotion on an item, the difference as a discount was directly sent to the savings jar. Here's the magical property of **"BUY WHOLESALE!!!"**

Wholesale shopping also applies to household chemical goods in concentrates. Initially, it may seem like you're paying more, but in reality, it lasts longer and ends up being cheaper.

"REGULAR CUSTOMER" - Look at what you regularly spend money on, find professionals, and become their regular customer: hair salon, dentist, car service, gym, massage, household appliances, café, restaurant. Become recognizable to them. You'll start hearing: "We know, we know. Discounts for you!" or "We have a special promotion for you today; you can pay later and at wholesale prices!" And when you bring a friend, they'll say, "Your discount for them, and a new client for us!"

"RECORD IT" - Simply keep a journal of income and expenses. Money comes in—record it. Money goes out—record it!

- You can choose to do absolutely nothing: no jars, no lists, no discounts, no wholesale. Just write down how much came in and how much went out for a year. At the end of the year, calculate the total, and that's it.))) Either you'll go crazy, or you'll start managing your money when you see how much money you gave away to others during the year. Don't forget to add another 20% to that amount.)))

You don't need to do anything but record. After a year—calculate! Statistics say that the average person spends $20,000 a year. Multiply that by 30–40%. That's $6,000–$8,000. Over five, ten years of accumulating and investing, friends, you're millionaires. But only with **a shopping act**—these are your millions. Without it, they're the millions of some guy who needs your millions more.))) Either you'll be happy, or that guy will create new jobs. Both are beneficial, but for the younger generation, unfortunately, it's a lesson in *"HOW NOT TO LIVE."* The choice is yours alone!

Save

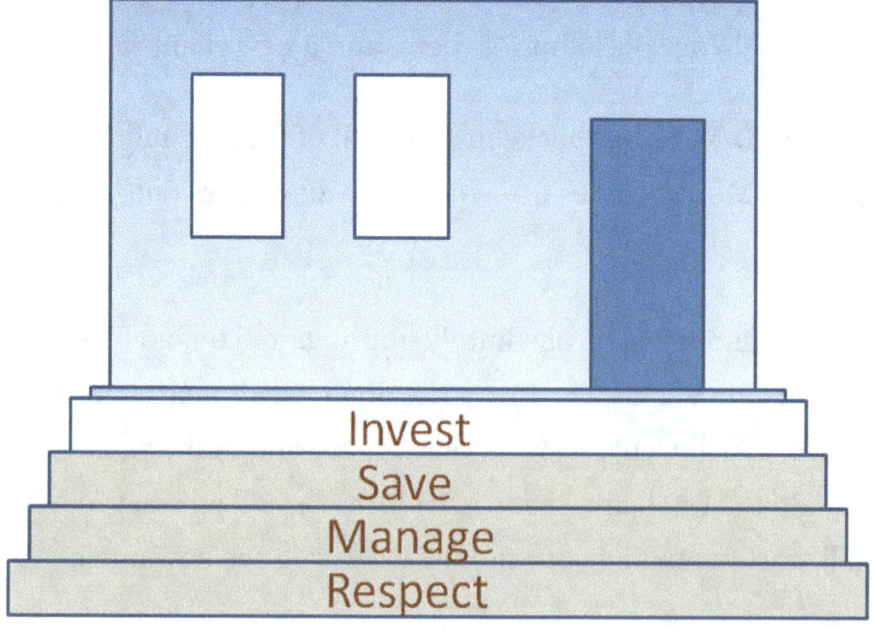

SAVINGS PROGRAM

1. Start a **PIGGY BANK**;
2. **DAILY** – Small Amount (ideally *$1 to the piggy bank*);
3. Upon receiving **INCOME** – *10% into the piggy bank*;
4. For **UNEXPECTED INCOME** – *50% into the piggy bank*;
5. Discounts **RECEIVED** – *100% to the piggy bank*;
6. When **SHOPPING** – *5%* (of the total purchase) *to the piggy bank*;
7. All **LOOSE CHANGE** – *100% to the piggy bank*;

- **First step – GET A PIGGY BANK: Recommendation:** – It can be a simple cardboard box, even a shoebox. The key is that it's not transparent. Secure the lid slightly so it can be easily opened at the end of the month, and cut a slot for money. You can decorate the box with your artistic skills, draw treasures, or simply write "My Financial Freedom" – though that's entirely optional.
- **Second step – EMOTIONALLY INSIGNIFICANT AMOUNT:** Let it be $1 at the start. The amount itself isn't as important as the act of putting it in the piggy bank every day. Anticipating the question: Can you put $30 in at once for the entire month and not worry? – You can, but doing it daily builds a habit. Imagine your habit as a little kitten you want to grow in a month so it knows

where to go to the toilet and becomes more fun to play with. You buy food for a month wholesale, but you're too lazy to feed it daily, so you decide to cram all the food into its mouth at once. What will happen? The same thing will happen to a financial habit if you build it monthly instead of daily! It's all about the habit, not the money. The habit is your kitten. Feed it with actions, and it grows; forget to feed it, and it dies. What becomes a habit works automatically.

- **Third step: – TEN PERCENT OF INCOME:** "Pay yourself first" – If you've read the book "The Richest Man in Babylon," you know this is the first rule of Babylon. For us, it's the primary habit: pay *yourself 10%, your future self 10%,* and only then the stores, then expenses. *Pay yourself 10% first.* Let's use visualization as an example.

Imagine yourself as two people: the present you and the future you. You've received your paycheck, come home joyful, planning treats, already mentally spending it, and drooling over the upcoming feast. You rush into the bathroom, and there's future you, with gray hair, looking at present you and asking:

– What are you doing here? – I just want to wash my hands, change, and head to the stores!

– Did you put 10% in the piggy bank? Did you put a dollar in the piggy bank this morning? Did you think about me? Get out of here until you do; stay dirty, just as you want to leave me dirty in the future!

You think, "Next month, for sure, I'll start saving for my future self, but now I've already planned my treats, even got the smell in my nose. I'll start next month or next year." You go to eat without washing your hands, change clothes, and head to the stores. You step into the kitchen, and there's future you again, sitting at the table, eating everything you prepared. Surprised, you ask:

– Did you already put 10% of your paycheck in the piggy bank, and do you put a dollar in every day for me?

Present you stands there blinking, thinking of treats, and future you raises their voice:

– Get out of the kitchen! If you're thinking only about treats and want to leave me starving, then no treats for you! Put 10% in the piggy bank, and then, by all means, come and eat.

Fourth Step – FIFTY PERCENT OF UNEXPECTED INCOME.

Surely, you've had situations where money came to you completely unexpectedly: a gift, a token of gratitude for helping someone, or even finding a decent bill on the street. With such income, fifty percent goes directly to the piggy bank, while the other half is for treating yourself. Did you have plans for a personal purchase in your monthly shopping list? Fulfill them.

For me, this step is more detailed. You know, when lending money, only lend free money—the funds you consider for unforeseen expenses. You decide the amount. Another rule about loans: if you lend money, forget about it. **Never pressure with questions like "When will you return it?"** It's better not to lend at all. When such loans are returned to me, I immediately send 50% to the piggy bank.)) Why is it necessary to treat yourself, your parents, spouse, or child with a gift? Because the body remembers this joy, and later, your subconscious will find unexpected funds itself.

Fifth Step – DISCOUNTS.

How often have you heard a conversation like this:

"Yesterday, I bought such amazing boots in the supermarket; they gave me a $25 discount, can you imagine? And then I used that $25 to buy…"

Do you think she saved or just thought she did? Here's an example:

Imagine you're talking to a friend, and he's boasting:

"Yesterday, I saved $5 on my way to work."

"How so?"

"I ran after the bus instead of riding it."

And you reply:

"Oh, David, tomorrow run after a taxi, and you'll save $80!"

Discounts are a fun game; start playing it, and I guarantee perpetual summer in your soul. Nowadays, shopping centers often display two prices, for instance:

"What's the price of this shirt that seems to adore me?"

"$150, but we'll sell it to you for $135 since it's part of a promotion. Generally, we sell these shirts for $220."

You calmly try it on, and the shirt hugs you and doesn't want to let you go. You realize it's yours and budgeted for that amount. Smiling pleasantly (remembering your savings program and the "DISCOUNT" section), you say:

"I really like it, thank you. But you forgot to write on the tag that for David, on Thursdays, the discount on this shirt is down to $125."

"Oh, there's already a $15 discount on this shirt; it's $150, but we're giving it to you for $135 as part of a promotion."

You smile even wider.

"Oh, I was so captivated by the shirt that I didn't hear about the discount. I only saw the two prices, and I liked $135. But I'd love to charm you and the shirt with a radiant smile, and the price will transform to $130. Today's a day of magic; let's make a miracle together!"

You sincerely smile, count out the money, thank them, take your purchase, and immediately set aside $20 in the secret pocket of your wallet, a substitute piggy bank. This substitute gets filled with discounts, 50% of unexpected income, one dollar (if forgotten in the morning), and 10% as soon as you receive money. Upon arriving home, unload the substitute, putting everything into the piggy bank.

Remember your future self? This isn't your money; it's your future self's money, i.e., someone else's. Return what's not yours before the little dragon named **BUY USELESS STUFF** devours it. Remember that girl named Inflation? When people hold their heads and sing a sad tune: Inflation, inflation, how do we escape it? It's not inflation you need to save from, *but yourself,* from that gluttonous little dragon. Inflation wouldn't even reach it; if it relied on us, there'd be no inflation in our country—it'd starve to death.

Sixth Step – PURCHASE TAX.

This is the most intriguing step. At all production facilities, salaries are taxed for everything imaginable, even shoes because they wear down the asphalt that will be laid next year.))) The most interesting part is that supermarkets also include VAT on price tags, meaning that the tax the store owner should pay is actually paid by the customer, who has already paid all other taxes. And tell me, does the tax administration ask your opinion before introducing new taxes? Therefore, introduce your own tax on your purchases, for your future self, without asking anyone. For myself, I designated 5% of all purchases. I come home, record all purchases in a program, calculate 5%, and like a strict tax administrator, take that amount from my wallet and transfer it to the piggy bank, THAT'S IT!!!

This step gets even more interesting when you include family creativity. For example, a husband wants to quit smoking; you agree: if he smokes, he puts $1 in the piggy bank. If he wants to fix his language, every swear word costs $1-$5 in the piggy bank. Wants to drink beer? Drink as much as you want, but every half-liter equals $1 in the piggy bank. Drink, smoke, swear... it's up to him.))) Either he'll stop swearing, drinking, and smoking, or you'll quickly become a millionaire.))

Seventh Step – SPARE CHANGE.

Have you ever observed your wallet? It's the perfect incubator for growing spare change, from pennies to dollars. In the morning, you empty the wallet of all change, only to find it full again by evening. What do we do with it? That's right, all the change goes directly into the piggy bank. Come home, unload the substitute piggy bank, and add all the spare change to the piggy bank. By the end of the month, you'll be amazed at how much change has accumulated.

Now, I'll reveal a SECRET. Your financial freedom begins with the piggy bank. Follow the steps strictly for a month, fill the piggy bank, and at the end of the month, open it, count the money, and invest it at compound interest (details on investments in various financial savings funds will follow). The next month, repeat the same steps, and again and again, without changing anything. Do you know what governs our lives? That's right, habits. Habits of thinking, habits of speaking, habits of doing, and as always, the usual results. This system develops the most essential habit: **The Financial Habit of Financial Freedom.**

The Property of Habit – A Very Important Point. A habit is formed in three stages and stays with you forever unless you replace it.

First Stage – *"At first – it's hard, unpleasant, and might even be painful."* For example, try getting used to alcoholic beverages in one day.))) How much would you need to drink to become an alcoholic? Try drinking all those liters in one day; it would definitely be hard, unpleasant, and even painful.)))

Second Stage – *"Then – it becomes easy, unnoticed, and even pleasant."*

Third Stage – you'll love it:

– Attention – ***The Habit Finds Money for Itself Automatically!!!***

How does it work? Have you ever seen a smoker run out of cigarettes and stop smoking? No, they will always find a way, even if not money for cigarettes, but the cigarettes themselves. The habit ensures they keep smoking.

Now, let's examine the financial habit of an average person. They earn $5,000 and spend all $5,000 in a month. Then they feel short of money and get a higher-paying job, earning $10,000, and spend all $10,000. Years go by, and they keep switching to better-paying jobs, earning $15,000, yet by the end of the month, they're at zero, having spent it all. What happens? More money, but the wallet is still empty at the end of the month. The answer is habit. **THE HABIT OF SPENDING MONEY, ALL OF IT, ALWAYS.** Their hands itch if the money isn't spent. They haven't even received the money yet, but it's already allocated in their mind to be spent entirely.

Freedom Strategy

"Invest"

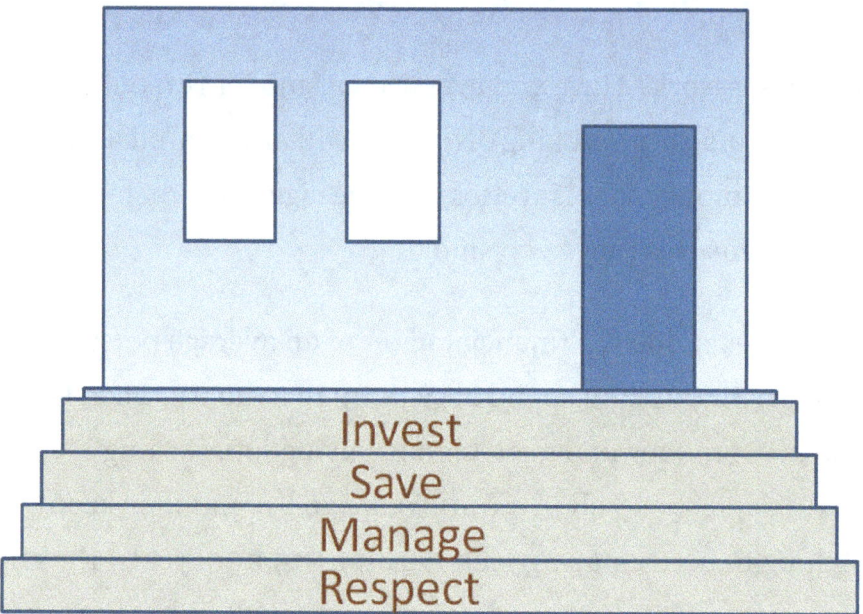

Do you want to know exactly how much money and what time frame you need to achieve your financial goals? What steps to take so that this amount and timeline become a reality? And feel confident that these steps are simple, easy, and something you already know how to do? Since this topic deals with investment and financial resource management, the word **"RISK"** will inevitably arise, elbowing out other terms. To address this, let's first define risk:

- **Risk** — a characteristic of a situation involving uncertainty of outcome, with the possibility of adverse consequences. In other words, it is the lack of certainty or inability to obtain reliable knowledge about a favorable outcome under given external circumstances. Thus, the term **RISK** can be succinctly defined as: **"RISK IS IGNORANCE"**!

For example, if you don't know how to drive a car but desperately want to, what should you do? Correct, you should learn to drive; otherwise, it's a risk both for you and for others.))) The same applies to financial investments. Have you heard the expression *"Invested and lost"?* This is why we will now delve into this **IMPORTANT** topic!

We already have money, don't we? Remember our piggy bank and how we learned to **RESPECT** money, then wisely **MANAGE** it, and carefully **SAVE** what wasn't spent? Now, let's discuss where to invest it.

- Did you know that in addition to financial capital, there is **"HUMAN CAPITAL"**? Here's its definition: **HUMAN CAPITAL** — *a combination of knowledge, skills, and abilities.* And remember, what is **RISK?** — it is **IGNORANCE**. But now we have both money and knowledge, and this dual capital needs to be **invested**. *Investing* isn't just about putting money somewhere; it's about **KNOWLEDGE.** Knowledge of what to do with this money and how to do it. Knowledge of where to start and knowledge of what the end result will be. In other words, **"INVESTING IS A PLAN."**

It is a plan for achieving the goal you have set. If your goal is financial security, then this is your **PLAN FOR FINANCIAL SECURITY.** If the goal is financial protection, then it's your **PLAN FOR FINANCIAL PROTECTION.** If the goal is financial independence, then it's your **PLAN FOR FINANCIAL INDEPENDENCE.** If you have a plan, you know exactly what, when, and how to do it, which is why:

PLAN = KNOWLEDGE

Freedom Strategy

"INVESTING IN FREEDOM"

1. **FREEDOM PROJECT**
2. **SECURITY PLAN**
3. **PROTECTION PLAN**
4. **INDEPENDENCE PLAN**
5. **FREEDOM PLAN**

Would you like to learn how your piggy bank can make you as wealthy as your imagination allows? Yes, exactly, because imagination is the key tool for creating a *freedom strategy!* Strategy is a realm of *practical activity* and is revealed only in *practical actions.*

1. The **FREEDOM PROJECT** is our goal! What do you think needs to be done to hit the target?

- Exactly, you need to have a target!))) In other words, you need to see the target, know the target – this is both **VISION and KNOWLEDGE**, both **PICTURE and NUMBERS.**

Now let's transition to action using an example. You want to live in your own house. In which city do you want to buy it, and how much does it cost? Suppose you want a house by the sea, and its price is **$3,200,000.** We know the price of your house; now we need to calculate how much money is spent monthly on its upkeep: gas, electricity, utilities, and its depreciation, i.e., the wear and tear on the house and its property because there's always something that needs fixing or repairing in the house, right? Let's calculate the house depreciation using the formula assuming the house will last for 50 years))) Divide the house price by the depreciation period: **$3,200,000 / 50 = $64,000 per year.** Now calculate the monthly payments by dividing the resulting sum by 12 months:

$64,000 / 12 = $5,333 per month.

Include other expenses here: exotic plants, household chemicals, maybe hiring someone to handle laundry and ironing. How much more will that add per month? – Let's add another **$2,500.** Combine this with the monthly house payment of $5,333, and the total becomes **$7,833.** If you have an **ASSET** that brings you this amount monthly, you can confidently move into such a house without worrying about where to get the money.

Next, your house certainly won't be empty; it will have various furniture, household appliances that do laundry, cook food, wash dishes, etc., and various electronics to play music and tell bedtime stories, right? – Let's calculate: suppose this setup costs **$600,000** and will serve us for seven years. Again, we calculate using the formula, dividing the total amount by the depreciation period:

$600,000 / 7 = $85,714 per year. Now calculate monthly by dividing the resulting sum by twelve months:

$85,714 / 12 = $7,143 per month.

Let's create a **DREAM TABLE** and write down our goals there

Dream	Price of a Dream	Expenses for a Dream
Dream Home	3 200 000	7 833
Comfort in Home	600 000	7 143
Dream (total)		14 976

Now, as a financially secure person, you need to decide how you will travel to work or for other errands: by tram, bus, or personal car? If it's a personal car, let's calculate its cost, depreciation, and monthly expenses: let's assume the car costs **$35,000.** Cars usually don't last more than six years without breakdowns on the roads. Let's substitute this into our formula and calculate:

$35,000 / 6 years = $5,834. Divide this by 12 months:

$5,834 / 12 months = $486 per month.

Add the monthly fuel cost, averaging $600, and the total becomes **$1,086.**

Let's add this to the table:

Dream	Price of a Dream	Expenses for a Dream
Dream Home	3 200 000	7 833
Comfort in Home	600 000	7 143
Dream car	35 000	1 086
Dream (total)		16 062

Now you have a house, a car, and assets to pay for all of it. What will you do? Not going to work, of course, because your assets cover all your passive needs. You'll do something you truly enjoy, something fascinating and captivating.

Let's assume this activity will cost approximately **$10,000**, and its monthly maintenance will be $370. Let's add it to the table:

Dream	Price of a Dream	Expenses for a Dream
Dream Home	3 200 000	7 833
Comfort in Home	600 000	7 143
Dream car	35 000	1 086
A job to my liking	10 000	370
Dream (total)		16 432

Take a look at what you already have: You live in a beautiful house with comfortable and stylish furniture, helpful appliances, and top-notch electronics. You drive a comfortable car for errands, you're engaged in your favorite activity, and all these pleasures are paid for by the assets you created, bringing you a monthly income of **$16,432**. However, it doesn't seem ethical to enjoy all these blessings without clothing, does it? The assets only cover the house, car, and your favorite activity, but you need to eat at least once a week and wear socks, don't you? So, let's calculate and add food and clothing expenses to the plan. Referring to statistical data, the average monthly food expense is **$1,000** per person. Let's also add $1,000 per month for personal items. Add this to the table.

Dream	Price of a Dream	Expenses for a Dream
Dream Home	3 200 000	7 833
Comfort in Home	600 000	7 143
Dream car	35 000	1 086
A job to my liking	10 000	370
Tasty Life	-	1 000
Personal Items	-	1 000
Dream (total)		18 432

I think you'll agree with me that in the wonderful life we're creating for ourselves, everything should be excellent. This includes looking great, which means being healthy, energetic, cheerful, smiling, and confident. This requires visits to the gym, beauty salons, tanning studios, and makeup artists. How much will you allocate for these needs monthly? Approximately $1,200. Add this to the table as another item.

Dream	Price of a Dream	Expenses for a Dream
Dream Home	3 200 000	7 833
Comfort in Home	600 000	7 143
Dream car	35 000	1 086
A job to my liking	10 000	370
Tasty Life	-	1 000
Personal Items	-	1 000
Favorite body	-	1 200
Dream (total)		19 632

Now for another point: despite all financial control, there will always be small expenses, so we must calculate and include this in the table. For instance, visiting guests and buying gifts, helping aging parents with presents or assistance, pocket expenses — these situations always arise. Let's estimate this at about **$4,000.** Add this to the freedom project table.

Dream	Price of a Dream	Expenses for a Dream
Dream Home	3 200 000	7 833
Comfort in Home	600 000	7 143
Dream car	35 000	1 086
A job to my liking	10 000	370
Tasty Life	-	1 000
Personal Items	-	1 000
Favorite body	-	1 200
Little nothings of life		4 000
Dream (total)		23 632

Continuing this serious topic, we need to calculate how much money we need monthly, or rather how much our assets should bring in each month to live freely. To do this, let's draw a picture of the required items and quantify them. Now tell me, are there places on our planet you've never visited but would like to? Let's calculate: how many times a year will you travel, and how much will it cost? Let's say you travel twice a year, costing **$5,000** per trip. Add this very necessary and personally enriching item to the table. Additionally, you might attend seminars for self-development. How often and what's the cost? Let's say each seminar costs $300, and you attend three annually, totaling **$900.** Remember the formula for calculations? Sum everything and write it down.

$5,900 / 12 = $492 per month

Dream	Price of a Dream	Expenses for a Dream
Dream Home	3 200 000	7 833
Comfort in Home	600 000	7 143
Dream car	35 000	1 086
A job to my liking	10 000	370
Tasty Life	-	1 000
Personal Items	-	1 000
Favorite body	-	1 200
Little nothings of life	-	4 000
Beautiful life	-	492
Dream (total)		24 124

Now let's add one more item to our table: Do you enjoy helping others? Sometimes, not everyone's life turns out as wonderfully as yours, and some may truly need your help. Wouldn't it feel good to know you can help? Think of the amount you can allocate for this purpose and add it as a very fulfilling and effective item in the table: **"To the giver, it shall be given and multiplied!"** I'll record $1,000 here and mark it in the table. You can write down your amount, whatever you can manage; you'll likely increase it when you see how effective this point is in reality.

Dream	Price of a Dream	Expenses for a Dream
Dream Home	3 200 000	7 833
Comfort in Home	600 000	7 143
Dream car	35 000	1 086
A job to my liking	10 000	370
Tasty Life	-	1 000
Personal Items	-	1 000
Favorite body	-	1 200
Little nothings of life	-	4 000
Beautiful life	-	492
Charity	-	1 000
Dream (total)		25 124

Remember, at the start of this topic, we discussed the freedom project: a **PICTURE and NUMBERS.** We now have the numbers in the table, and the picture is our vision of what we truly want. Now we need one final element: **TIME.** Yes, exactly that. We need time to enjoy all these blessings; otherwise, everything calculated and written down in the table can be crossed out right now with a bold red marker. To have both money and time, we need **CAPITAL.**

Capital that generates an income of **$25,124 per month.** Unlike a business, capital provides both time and money. **Investing** is about allocating capital: deposit money and receive interest. Remember our piggy bank? There's your answer to where to find money for monthly investments. We solved this task, and now we know we need capital and where to get it. The only thing left is to calculate the required capital and add it as the final item in our table.

Let's assume the bank pays an annual interest rate of 12%. Divide this percentage by 12 months to get 1% per month. Now divide our required monthly income, $25,124, by 0.01:

$25,124 / 0.01 = $2,512,400

Our dream capital is **$2,512,400**, generating a monthly income of **$25,124**, fully covering all our desires!

Dream	Price of a Dream	Expenses for a Dream
Dream Home	3 200 000	7 833
Comfort in Home	600 000	7 143
Dream car	35 000	1 086
A job to my liking	10 000	370
Tasty Life	-	1 000
Personal Items	-	1 000
Favorite body	-	1 200
Little nothings of life	-	4 000
Beautiful life	-	492
Charity	-	1 000
Dream (total)		25 124
Dream Capital	Bank interest = 1% month	2 512 400

But it would seem that's all, but there's still one more question. We have created a **financial freedom project:** we have a picture of the lifestyle we want to live, and we have a number—the size of the capital that financially guarantees this lifestyle. But we have not yet considered one more factor: INFLATION. Solving this issue is very simple.))) Imagine that your capital is constantly growing, as if increasing itself by exactly the same percentage that inflation consumes from money every year. Can you imagine that? Now let's, as always, simplify everything: suppose the annual inflation rate is 12%, which means one percent per month. This means our capital must grow by 1% per month. Looking at our dream capital, which amounts to

$2,512,400, we see that monthly it equals **$25,124.** This is the amount by which our capital must grow for our DREAM CAPITAL to amount to:

(2,512,400 + 2,512,400 = $5,024,800)

Now this is our DREAM CAPITAL, as this amount is sufficient to cover all our expenses and offset inflation.

Dream	Price of a Dream	Expenses for a Dream
Dream Home	3 200 000	7 833
Comfort in Home	600 000	7 143
Dream car	35 000	1 086
A job to my liking	10 000	370
Tasty Life	-	1 000
Personal Items	-	1 000
Favorite body	-	1 200
Little nothings of life	-	4 000
Beautiful life	-	492
Charity	-	1 000
Dream (total)		25 124
Dream Capital	Bank interest = 1% month	5 024 800

Now, everything is ready. The FREEDOM PROJECT is complete; we have the picture, which is on the left in our table, and we have the numbers. Remember, FREEDOM PROJECT = PICTURE + NUMBERS! This number is now our goal, which means our goal is capital amounting to **$5,024,800.**

I want to point out that in this topic, we calculated and created capital that covers our monthly expenses and inflation, but it does not include money for buying a house, home comforts, a car, or a passion project. We'll talk about that later. But for now, let me ask you: Are you interested in where to find capital amounting to **$5,024,800?**))) Then let's move on to the next topic.

Security Plan

So, our goal is **capital amounting to $5,024,800**, and only four steps separate us from this goal. These four steps are our four plans:

1. **SECURITY PLAN**
2. **PROTECTION PLAN**
3. **INDEPENDENCE PLAN**
4. **FREEDOM PLAN**

- **SECURITY PLAN** – What is this plan? It is a life without danger. Let's assume we have created capital, placed it, and it generates interest for us. But what if this capital disappears? It would mean all our dreams go down the drain. Therefore, we need to place this capital *SECURELY, VERY SECURELY*, right? But where? Banks? Trust in banks, to put it mildly, leaves much to be desired. But this low reliability only exists when all capital is stored in one place. Let's recall that when signing a deposit agreement, in force majeure circumstances, the bank guarantees payment (for example, up to $50,000). So, to minimize risks, the capital must be distributed among several banks. Let's calculate: our capital amounts to **$5,024,800**. Divide it by **$50,000**, and we get **100** banks.))) It turns out there won't be enough banks in the whole country. This means we need to invest in other financial structures, but with greater reliability.

The Security Plan, apart from preserving the capital we created, includes the function of protecting our actions throughout the period while we create our **DREAM CAPITAL** from all eventualities and mistakes. Remember the definition of risk? Risk assumes uncertainty or the inability to obtain *reliable knowledge* about the favorable outcome of a planned event. Our security plan is designed to provide exactly **RELIABLE KNOWLEDGE** about the favorable outcome of the planned event. After all, we are not planning small change; we are planning our **LIFE!**

Favorable events – We follow the security plan, and we achieve a favorable outcome!

Unfavorable events – We follow the security plan, and we still achieve a *favorable outcome)))* because our plan foresees reaching the goal under **any circumstances.** Of course, it's impossible to foresee everything, but we can exclude certain events from the list of risks, such as when we use financial institutions other than banks, for example: - Insurance accumulation companies specializing in a particular type of insurance. **THE SECURITY PLAN** is the safety of the path to dream capital and the safety of ***DREAM CAPITAL*** once it's created.

What is an insurance accumulation company? It's a hybrid of an insurance company and a bank. This means you can get both money and interest without jumping through hoops to get your funds because you'll receive everything regardless. Moreover, policies can be issued in any currency, and the interest on invested capital is usually higher than in banks. Policy payments are made annually, usually starting from $1,000. The term depends on age and is calculated with a consultant; there's no need to go into details here. What do we do? We find a financial consultant from the company of interest and select the appropriate accumulation program. For example, you choose an accumulation program for 10 years with an annual payment of $2,000. Where to get money for the payment every year if your monthly salary is only $2,500? – Correct, the piggy bank!))) Our capital is our piggy bank. With an income of $2,500 per month, you'll definitely have $400 or more each month. Open a deposit account in the bank for a year with monthly replenishment, and at the end of each month, transfer the entire contents of the piggy bank to this deposit. After a year, with monthly deposits of $400, you'll have an amount of $5,200 or more in your account. Withdraw $2,000 and pay for the insurance policy, and reinvest the remaining amount in a new one-year deposit, repeating the process. This way, you'll already have two investment programs that will preserve and grow your **DREAM CAPITAL plus security!**

Perhaps someone reading this material, like me, had a negative attitude toward insurance companies. It often happened that I was more frequently scared with fears instead of being shown the benefits of capital investment. After mastering the system of investing and the art of spending money, I now fully support the statement: - If you are a **responsible adult,** the **breadwinner** in the family, *you simply have no right to leave the house without insurance because, by doing so, you expose your closest and dearest people to risk!*

The main thing to understand in the security program is this: - The program is created not for **PROFIT** but for **RELIABILITY.** Profit will come from other plans.

The task of this program does not include advertising campaigns.)))

Protection Plan

Protection Plan:

- The formula is DP = expenses (monthly) * (6 - 12).

The numbers in parentheses (6-12) represent the months, and you can decide the duration yourself. The Protection Plan is a reserve for six months or more. The essence of this plan is simple: just like in life, finances have their seasons. You will experience summers and winters—times when money is abundant and times when it is scarce. What happens when you're in the summer of your finances? You get used to spending comfortably. But when winter arrives—you're asked to leave your job or your business falters—what happens then? Instead of focusing 80% of your time on fixing the business or finding a new, profitable job, you'll spend that time scrambling to find $2,000-$3,000 to cover basic living expenses: feeding your children, paying for kindergarten or music school. If you lack a **"PROTECTION PLAN"**, you'll make rash decisions, feel anxious, and spiral into further losses and debts. Winter will slowly turn into an ice age.

You likely know people who once ran successful businesses but went bankrupt. Do you know why? Now you do: they didn't have a **PROTECTION PLAN!**

But if you have a six-month or longer reserve of funds, then even if you lose your job or your business fails, you can sit down calmly and say to yourself:

"Relax, my friend, don't panic. What are our monthly expenses? Ah, $1,500. And we have $9,000. That means for six whole months, every single day, we'll have 24 hours of free time. So let's take our time to figure out what went wrong, craft a new action plan, and in half a year, we'll either start a new business or find a new job."

Six months is the minimum reserve for a **PROTECTION PLAN**. Calculate your monthly expenses, multiply by 6, and you'll get the amount needed for your **PROTECTION PLAN.** These funds are best stored in a bank. Find a reliable bank, open an account, and accumulate this amount there. If you already have this sum, deposit it in the bank and don't touch it:

THIS IS AN UNTENABLE RESERVE, to be used only in emergencies, only when winter arrives.))) ***The funds in the PROTECTION PLAN must be liquid, i.e., quickly accessible.*** For this purpose, a bank is one of the best tools available.

Money for the protection plan isn't a problem; we take it from the piggy bank because we are responsible adults who remember our future selves and diligently follow the **"SAVINGS PROGRAM"**. Imagine that we take $1,000 from the piggy bank each month and deposit it into a secure financial institution. The interest might not be high, but it's reliable. Let's assume 12% annually (1% monthly). Refer to the illustration to see what happens.

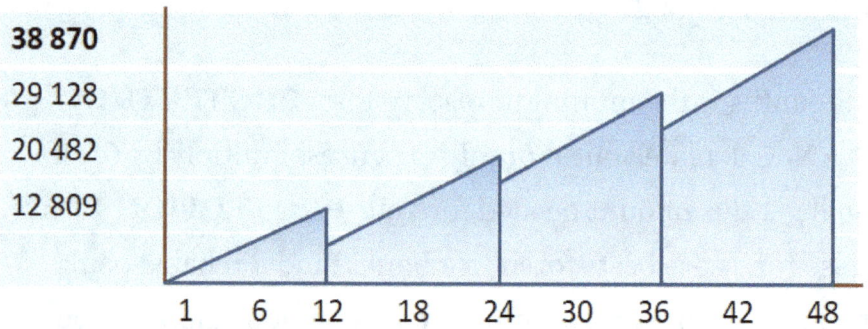

On the horizontal axis, we have months, and on the vertical axis, the total accumulated amount over the year as we set aside $1,000 monthly from the piggy bank. Note that at the start of each year, the graph shows a slight dip. Why? Because once a year, at a specific time, we need to pay for the insurance savings policy. That's why we withdraw these funds from the **PROTECTION PLAN.** By following the Savings Program, we automatically accomplish two additional goals: the **SECURITY PLAN** and the **PROTECTION PLAN!!!**

This system ensures we never stress about where to find the money. We always have funds both to pay for the insurance savings policy and to build the protection plan. Looking at the graph, you'll notice that by the end of the fourth year, our **PROTECTION PLAN** is fully completed.

Let's move on to the next point.

Independence Plan

Let's look at the formula:

Independence Plan = Expenses (month) / % (month)

Independence Plan is the capital sum calculated based on monthly expenses.

Expenses (month) – This refers to our monthly expenses.

% (month) – This refers to the average monthly bank interest.

Our Independence Plan requires **$2,500 per month:**

- Inputting these figures into the formula gives us:

$2,500 / 0.01 = $250,000.

This means that when we deposit $250,000 in a bank with a 12% annual interest rate (or 1% monthly), we will receive $2,500 monthly in interest, covering our expenses. Hence, this is called the **Independence Plan.**

By continuing to set aside **$1,000** monthly, in 11 years, we'll accumulate **$278,334.** Now consider this: adding the **Protection Plan** (4 years) to the Independence Plan (11 years), the total timeline is 15 years. While 15 years may seem short in the grand scheme of the universe, it's significant in human life. This begs the question: Can it be faster?

- Of course, it can. We take $1,000 monthly from the piggy bank—funds that our little dragon **"Buy Useless Stuff"** couldn't snatch from us. Now, by consciously increasing monthly contributions to **$2,000,** the timeline shortens to 7 years, resulting in **$268,571**. This is better but still feels long; we want results "yesterday." At this point, it's worth remembering that other financial tools, like Mutual Investment Funds (MIFs), offer higher returns (up to 24% annually) than banks, albeit with higher risks. Familiarize yourself with MIFs; there's plenty of information online. Once comfortable, consider purchasing certificates from such funds. Now, by increasing our monthly contributions to **$2,000** and annual interest to 24%, let's see what happens: **$2,000 monthly at 24% compounding = $239,227 (in 5 years).** The picture starts to look much brighter.)))

Now, let's move on to the most exciting plan:

Freedom Plan

Freedom Plan Formula:

Freedom Plan = Month / % (month)

Freedom Plan refers to the capital sum calculated based on our dream monthly expenses.

Month – This represents the monthly cost of our dream lifestyle. Remember we calculated it to be **$50,248 per month.**

% (month) – This is the average monthly bank interest rate.

Substituting our figures into the formula gives us:

50,248 / 0.01 = $5,024,800.

This calculation gives us the **DREAM CAPITAL** amount, which we've already recorded in the **"FREEDOM PROJECT" table.** What's next? We develop a new plan, beginning with calculating how to achieve this sum. By continuing with the Independence Plan (setting aside **$2,000 monthly at 24% compounding),** we calculate the time required to reach this goal. (Use a compound interest calculator available online.) The exciting news: in 17 years, we will have accumulated **$5,806,379.**

While this number is pleasing, the timeline feels discouraging. Why does it seem like we always want results "NOW" or even "YESTERDAY"? Think about it: how many people do you know who, after 17 years of work, achieve **FINANCIAL FREEDOM** before official retirement? Believe me, it's still better than becoming a billionaire at 100.

You can reduce this timeline by calculating how much more you can set aside monthly. Input these numbers into the calculator to see how much sooner you can achieve your **DREAM.**

I'll demonstrate figures for **$10,000 monthly contributions.** This sum can be achieved by mastering and increasing earnings during the Independence Plan phase.

Remember, in our "house for money," there's another topic, **"CREATE,"** which we'll explore later. For now, it's **CRUCIAL** to consolidate this material. Let's proceed:

1. Develop the **"FREEDOM PROJECT"** – Create a vision of your dream life and calculate its cost.
2. Develop the **"SECURITY PLAN"** – Build a safety corridor to protect against foreseeable uncertainties.
3. Develop the **"PROTECTION PLAN"** – By the end of year four, this plan is fully funded. Each month, withdraw $1,000 from the piggy bank and deposit it into a financial institution at 12% annual compound interest.
4. Develop the **"INDEPENDENCE PLAN"** – By mastering mutual investment funds and achieving 24% annual returns, setting aside **$2,000 monthly** will fulfill the Independence Plan in 5 years.
5. Develop the **"FREEDOM PLAN"** – Setting aside **$10,000 monthly** at 24% annual returns will achieve Financial Freedom in 11 years. Over the next 13 years, you'll realize your goals.

Let's now explore ways to accelerate this process and move to the next topic!

Create

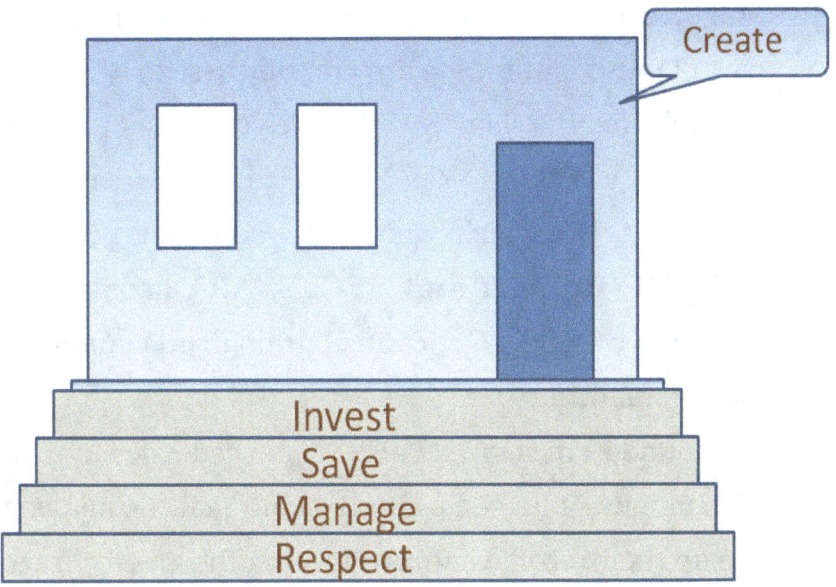

In this topic, we will discuss increasing income. Let's revisit our **"FINANCIAL FREEDOM"** house and see that the foundation has grown significantly stronger:

- We have examined the slab of the foundation **"RESPECT,"** and now we know how to change our attitude toward money using the *"Investment Table."* We understand how a dollar grows if it's not just spent but wisely invested. We've grasped how money works and its true **PURPOSE** — *to Serve Humanity!*

- We studied the slab **"MANAGE,"** and now we know how to handle money correctly using the **"PURCHASE ACT"** technique. We've taken control of the most unruly type of expense related to maintaining our chosen **LIFESTYLE.** By controlling our costs (taming the dragon called ***"Buy Useless Stuff"***), we can redirect part of our cash flow toward creating assets.
- By exploring the slab **"SAVE,"** we've learned to create our personal ***"SAVINGS PROGRAM"*** (remember the PIGGY BANK), which, when followed regularly, builds such **IMPORTANT and NECESSARY** habits as saving what we've managed to control through good money management!
- The foundation slab **"INVEST"** showed us what to do with money. It helped us understand that not all people use up their income entirely, feeding the greedy dragon. Some wisely think about what life could become if they rely only on the state. These individuals treat their earnings carefully and build savings. We haven't discovered America here; some people have always saved and still do.))) You might think your money is only yours, but in reality, it's always being hunted; there's always a big hunt for your money!

The most **IMPORTANT** lesson from **"INVEST"** is this: **Investing is a PLAN — a clear, accessible, well-thought-**

out plan. If it's complicated, it's not investing. Investing should be **SIMPLE!** Very simple, even boringly primitive, a straightforward set of repetitive actions leading to a set goal and becoming a **HABIT.** You perform simple tasks because you know they lead to your **DREAM.**

Simple actions, every day: - Expense notebook, piggy bank, bank once a month. Every day: expense notebook, piggy bank, bank once a month. Boring? Oh, very boring! Expenses - piggy bank, piggy bank - bank, once a year: Bank - insurance company. Again: expenses - piggy bank, piggy bank - bank, bank - insurance company. These silly actions are repeated, repeated, and repeated. At first, it feels boring, but soon you don't even notice; you don't think about it. IT works on its own because it becomes a **HABIT.** That's why it should become a habit—so you can do it without noticing. Remember: *"Later, it's easy, unnoticed, and even pleasant"?* That's why investing must be simple and boring, and the **PLAN** must make it **CORRECT!**

When the habit takes over spending, saving, and investing, your body no longer distracts your attention. The habit controls your thoughts, and you always know you have money. Your mind knows it and has adapted. How does it now think? - Correctly: *"There's money, there's a lot of money; where to invest?"* Remember who thinks this way?

Now let's look at our strategy from a different perspective and find clues for speeding things up. What plans do we need to create and execute to become financially free? - *"Safety," "Protection," "Independence," and "Freedom" Plans.*

Now let's consider business. But we need not just any business but a **BUSINESS SYSTEM** — a business set up to run without your presence. Let's imagine we already have such a business. Now we need a strategy to ensure this business quickly leads us to freedom. Imagine you discover a business still in its box—a construction kit needing assembly, adjustment, and launching to work independently. Let's say it's a pastry kiosk. There's a primary company that makes these pastries and also produces the kiosks. You sign a contract, find a busy location for the kiosk, and purchase it for **$20,000** (all figures are hypothetical). You set it up in a great spot and hire a seller for **$1,500 per month** to sell the pastries. The company delivers ready-made pastries daily to the kiosks and collects the money and leftovers in the evening. Everything works without you: the company delivers and picks up goods, and the seller handles sales. This kiosk brings in **$5,000** in monthly net income, and the company transfers this amount to you at the end of each month per contract. Create a table to track how the kiosk operates and how we invest our income. Let's assume we start with no initial capital and save **$1,000 per month** while following our **"PROTECTION PLAN."**

Month	Investment	Beginning of month	Interest	End of month
1	1000	1 000	15	1 015
2	1000	2 015,00	30,23	2 045,23
3	1000	3 045,23	45,68	3 090,90
4	1000	4 090,90	61,36	4 152,27
5	1000	5 152,27	77,28	5 229,55
6	1000	6 229,55	93,44	6 322,99
7	1000	7 322,99	109,84	7 432,84
8	1000	8 432,84	126,49	8 559,33
9	1000	9 559,33	143,39	9 702,72
10	1000	10 702,72	160,54	10 863,26
11	1000	11 863,26	177,95	11 041,21
12	1000	13 041,21	195,62	13 236,83
13	1000	14 236,83	213,55	14 450,38
14	1000	15 450,38	231,76	15 682,14
15	1000	16 682,14	250,23	16 932,37
16	1000	17 932,37	268,99	17 201,36
17	1000	19 201,36	288,02	19 489,38
18	1000	20 489,38	307,34	20 796,72

We invest our savings at an annual rate of 18%, or 1.5% monthly. For eighteen months, we focus solely on this strategy, and during our free time, we read books on business and trade, attend seminars, and build connections in the field. During this period, we find a suitable company and a great location for our kiosk. Let's calculate how much money we've accumulated in these 18 months: **$20,796.** We recall that this amount is sufficient to launch a business system (set up a kiosk), which costs us **$20,000.**

We immediately sign a contract with the primary company, purchase, and launch the business. The kiosk operates independently, generating a monthly profit of **$5,000.** We remember that this amount is enough to launch a business system. Now, all net profits are reinvested, plus an additional **$1,000** from our savings.

In the 19th month, we invest only **$1,000** from our savings, plus **$796.72** (the remaining funds after purchasing the kiosk) since the kiosk's earnings are received only at the end of the month. We create a new table:

Month	Investment	Beginning of month	Interest	End of month
19	1 796,72	1 796,72	26,95	1 823,67
20	6 000	7 823,67	117,36	7 941,03
21	6 000	13 941,03	209,12	13 150,14
22	6 000	20 150,14	302,25	20 452,39

TOTAL KIOSKS = 1

In just four months, we accumulate enough funds to purchase another kiosk, as our account now holds **$20,452.** We buy a second kiosk, hire another employee, and now invest **$1,000** from savings plus two monthly profits of **$5,000** from both kiosks:

$1,000 + $5,000 + $5,000 = $11,000 monthly investments. We build the next table considering the remaining funds after purchasing the second kiosk and the income from the new kiosk at the end of the month:

Month	Investment	Beginning of month	Interest	End of month
23	7 452,39	7 452,39	111,79	7 564,18
24	11 000	18 564,18	278,46	18 842,64
25	11 000	29 842,64	447,64	30 290,28

TOTAL KIOSKS = 2

The table shows that money for a new kiosk accumulates in just three months. We purchase another kiosk, enabling monthly investments of **$15,000** (from three kiosks) plus **$1,000** from savings, totaling **$16,000** monthly. We create another table:

Month	Investment	Beginning of month	Interest	End of month
26	21 290,28	21 290,28	319,35	21 609,63

TOTAL KIOSKS = 3

Notice that from the 26th month onward, we can buy one kiosk every month. Let's extend our table to three years and see the results:

Month	Investment	Beginning of month	Interest	End of month
27	17 609,63	17 609,63	264,14	17 873,77
28	21 000	38 873,77	583,14	39 456,88

TOTAL KIOSKS = 4

By the 27th month, we do not purchase a kiosk, but by the 28th month, we need an additional **$543.22** to purchase two kiosks.

This issue can be resolved by borrowing from family. We buy two kiosks, and now we have **six kiosks** generating an income of **$30,000 monthly.** Remember, kiosk profitability begins in the second month of operation. After a month of work, the company pays us a contract-based reward of **$5,000.**

We create the next table:

Month	Investment	Beginning of month	Interest	End of month
29	20 000	20 000	300	20 300

TOTAL KIOSKS = 6

We purchase another kiosk and repay the borrowed amount of **$243.22** (the remainder from the previous month's purchase). Next table:

Month	Investment	Beginning of month	Interest	End of month
30	30 000	30 000	450	30 450

TOTAL KIOSKS = 7

We buy one more kiosk, repay the remaining **$243.22**, and update the table:

Month	Investment	Beginning of month	Interest	End of month
31	46 206,78	46 206,78	693,10	46 899,88

TOTAL KIOSKS = 8

Now, we have enough funds to purchase two additional kiosks. We update the table:

Month	Investment	Beginning of month	Interest	End of month
32	47 899,88	47 899,88	718,5	48 618,38

TOTAL KIOSKS = 10

By the end of the 32nd month, we've acquired 10 kiosks, generating a total monthly income of **$50,000**. From this point forward, we can purchase two kiosks every month. Let's extend the table to 36 months to build our network of kiosks (deliciousness):

Month	Investment	Beginning of month	Interest	End of month
33	49 618,38	49 618,38	744,28	50 362,66

TOTAL KIOSKS = 12

We purchase two more kiosks and update the table:

Month	Investment	Beginning of month	Interest	End of month
34	61 362,66	61 362,66	920,44	62 283,10

TOTAL KIOSKS = 15

We purchase three kiosks, achieving **15 kiosks with a monthly income of $75,000.** Next table:

Month	Investment	Beginning of month	Interest	End of month
35	63 283,10	63 283,10	949,25	64 232,35

TOTAL KIOSKS = 18

We purchase three more kiosks, reaching **18 kiosks with a monthly income of $90,000.** Next table:

Month	Investment	Beginning of month	Interest	End of month
36	80 232,35	80 232,35	1 203,49	81 435,84

TOTAL KIOSKS = 20

Summing Up Our Business

Over the three years of developing our business, here's what we've achieved:

- For the first 18 months, we saved up to purchase a franchise while attending business training sessions, networking with professionals, and studying business literature. Following the strategies outlined in our earlier chapters, we managed our finances diligently.
- As a result of our consistent efforts, after 18 months, we saved enough to purchase a franchise (a turnkey business system), which operates autonomously and generates monthly income.
- Over the next 18 months, we expanded our business system by sequentially acquiring kiosks, building a network of 20 kiosks that generate a **total monthly income of $100,000.** By the end of the 36th month, after purchasing the 20th kiosk, we still had a balance of **$41,435.84.**

Thus, in just three years, we built a **BUSINESS SYSTEM** that operates independently and provides a monthly income of **$100,000!!!**

These kiosks serve as an example. In reality, there are many franchise systems available, but their key feature is that, *if launched correctly, they operate without the owner's constant presence!*

Let's solidify this material because it is **VERY IMPORTANT!!!**

If this business excites you and you're determined to keep growing, let's say you decide to develop it further in other cities. This will be your homework: use your compound interest calculator to calculate your total monthly profit if, over the next year, you purchase and launch several kiosks each month in different cities.)))

Now let's remember that the goal of this combined program is to master the knowledge and strategy for achieving financial freedom, collectively referred to as the **"Building of Financial Freedom."**

Using kiosks as an example (don't rush to invest all your savings in purchasing them tomorrow—that could become an exclusive purchase of headaches), we've demonstrated how to create the desired cash flow that aligns with your goals in a shorter timeframe. Do you think the topic **"Business System"** is worth exploring to accelerate the creation of the **NECESSARY** cash flow? Let me emphasize this: understanding how a **BUSINESS SYSTEM** is launched, configured, managed, and how a **TEAM** is built to develop the system—how to train, motivate, and nurture them—is crucial. In a **BUSINESS SYSTEM, the true asset isn't the money or kiosks; it's the PEOPLE!!!**

Now, if you decide to personally control all the kiosks, calculate how many kiosks you have in different cities after four years. Then estimate the time needed daily for each kiosk, say 30 minutes. Multiply this by the number of kiosks, and you'll see that the required time exceeds 24 hours—you'd barely have time for a bathroom break, and no cosmetics can save someone who hasn't had one in four years.)))

Returning to the topic, after four years, we've created a business system that generates a substantial monthly income. Now, we can purchase everything outlined in our **"Freedom Project."** However, having completed business courses and training, we know that businesses have winters too. Some kiosks may need to close, but we've learned that **CAPITAL IS MORE RELIABLE THAN BUSINESS!** Thus, we decide to **"USE OUR BUSINESS TO BUILD CAPITAL."**

We already have income for living expenses, as we've completed the **PROTECTION PLAN** and **INDEPENDENCE PLAN**. We now decide to establish **"STOP EXPENSES!!!"** This means setting a fixed monthly spending limit beyond which you won't go. For instance, you decide that you won't spend more than *$50,000 monthly,* allocating the rest for investments in banks and mutual funds according to your **"FREEDOM PLAN."** It's now easy to calculate how long it will take to accumulate the necessary sum by dividing your target amount by your monthly investment, giving you the number of months needed to achieve your plan.

Calculate precisely how many years it will take—*it's crucial to quantify your plan.*

In general, this timeline averages four years for the **Freedom Plan** and four years for the **Protection Plan,** totaling eight years to achieve **FINANCIAL FREEDOM and YOUR DREAM.** Now, you decide to shorten this timeline by a year to become financially independent within seven years. Here's how:

You meet a successful and wealthy individual—someone you likely already know—and say something like this:

"Rockefeller Rockefellerovich, I'm delighted to know you—a wise, successful, and wealthy person from whom I've learned so much simply by observing your thoughts and actions. Knowing you has been an example of success and a model for emulation. You've helped me immensely on my journey as an entrepreneur and as a person. I would like to express my gratitude. An excellent idea has come to my mind, and if you have the time to listen, I'd gladly share how I could repay the wisdom you've shared with me."

You then propose selling your business system to them for a price slightly higher than its annual profit, explaining that their investment will yield a guaranteed 30% annual return after taxes—a higher rate than mutual funds offering 20-25%.

Summing Up:

- After selling your business system, you immediately receive the missing amount, which, when added to your existing funds, totals the amount outlined in the FREEDOM PLAN. By doing so, you reduce the timeline by one year! Now, you are a financially free individual. Let's take a look at how our journey appears in the illustration:

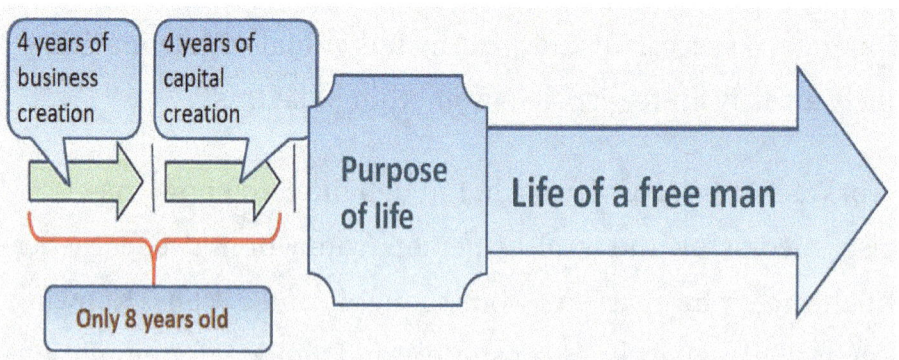

How do you like this story?

By mastering, creating, and utilizing the tool called the "Business System," we can implement all four plans in the shortest possible time, practically simultaneously. Moreover, the growth in business income significantly accelerates the achievement of our ultimate goal—the creation of **"DREAM CAPITAL."** Of course, creating a business system isn't easy; it requires experience, which can be gained by engaging in real entrepreneurial activities, ideally under the guidance of an experienced mentor.

Pay attention to the completeness of the picture of the **"Building of Financial Freedom."** This structure is a combination of educational and developmental activities that equip any individual with the skills, knowledge, and qualities needed to achieve **"Financial Freedom"** in the shortest possible time! Now, let's explore the secret formula that will guide us in the direction we need to work to become a person whose knowledge, skills, and qualities consistently increase financial flows!

ATTENTION

The Secret INCOME FORMULA

$I = P \times E \times D \times S \times I$

Where:

- **I — INCOME**

- **P — PROFESSIONALISM**
- **E — ENERGY POTENTIAL**
- **D — DEVELOPMENT**
- **S — SELF-ESTEEM**
- **I — IDEOLOGY**

The income formula can also be used as a test. By answering these questions, you immediately see what needs improvement and where to focus your efforts.)))

1. Professionalism:

You have a dream and a structured **"Freedom Project."** You have all the plans, and you simply execute them daily: an expense journal, a piggy bank, and a monthly trip to the bank. Initially, it's hard, but eventually, it becomes a habit.

Question 1: - Do you have a passion for your work? If not, score 1. If yes, score 10.

You might think, "I have a dream of growing beautiful grape varieties, but for now, I'm working a job to earn money. I enjoy my work and do it diligently," so you score 4.5.

Question 2: - How skilled are you in your current work?

If you're a complete beginner, score 1. If you're an expert constantly improving and recognized in your field, score 10.

"Let's see... I work for a great boss, can answer calls confidently, smile at the right moments, and even type with one finger! I'm paid $3,000 a month, so I'm not completely inexperienced." You score 3.

Question 3: - Do you have a mentor, and how professional is your mentor?

If you don't have one or your mentor lacks professionalism, score 1. If your mentor is the best in their field, demanding yet fair, and provides valuable guidance, score 10.

"Hmm... I don't have a mentor. I was shown the basics once, and I've been figuring things out on my own ever since. I really need a mentor who is both kind and strict, so I score 4.5."

Calculating Your PROFESSIONALISM SCORE:

Find the average by summing your scores and dividing by the number of questions:

1. Passion for work – 4.5
2. Skill level – 3
3. Mentor's professionalism – 4.5

(4.5 + 3 + 4.5) / 3 = 4

Not great, but it's a starting point. Let's move forward!

Moving on to the Next Point: "Energy Potential"

Question One:

- Can you give 100%, or even 101%, in your work? How much effort do you usually invest in what you do? How much of yourself do you put into the work in which you aim to become a professional?

Oh, how intriguing, you think. What does it mean to give your all? If you barely go through the motions, dragging your body from call to lunch break, that's 1 point.

But if you love your work, give it your all, the day flies by, and the people around you feel your energy and shine—10 points.

Hmm, a good question: how much effort do I put in? I go to work, chat about the news with colleagues, play a game on my phone, and let out a few colorful expressions. How much effort does that take? Well, I don't sleep on the job, I do my work diligently and on time, I know a lot of jokes, and people enjoy being around me. Alright, I'll give myself 7 points.

Question Two: How often do you feel tired, and how quickly do you recover?

If you wake up every day feeling exhausted, with life long lost its joy, and even a news anchor's voice derails your day, that's 1 point.

If you can quickly regain your calm, fully recharge after a few hours of sleep, and have the ability to push your body to its limits and then relax it on command, that's 10 points.

This one's easier. I'm not yet a workhorse, I get enough rest, I have plenty of energy, and there's room to grow. Modestly, I'll give myself 9 points.

Question Three: Do you regularly engage in physical activity?

If the last time you exercised was in the fifth grade when you ditched class, or if walking to the bathroom feels like a hike that requires a taxi, that's 1 point.

If you work out two to three times a week, filling your body with life and joy, and do an intense program once or twice a year that challenges your body and mind, that's 10 points.

Okay, I don't do many exercises—just a morning stretch to make brushing my teeth easier. Watching sports on TV counts, right? Modestly, I'll give myself 3.5 points.

2. "E" – ENERGY POTENTIAL:

- My energy – 7 points;
- Resilience – 9 points;
- Recovery ability – 3.5 points.

So it's not just about extracting benefits from your body and mind; you also need to invest in them. They say the first half of life, we work for our bodies; the second half, they work for us. Let's calculate the average:

(7 + 9 + 3.5) / 3 = 6.5.

3. Third Point: Development

An intriguing point—you'll soon see why.

Question One: How many people in your country know about the work you do, the company you work for, or the product you sell?

If nobody does what you do, and the idea just popped into your head; if no one has heard of your company, and you haven't even written its charter yet; if even you don't fully understand your product or service because it's still in its early stages, give yourself 1 point.

If your work is in demand by everyone in your country, your company is a household name, and people line up for your product or service, eagerly talking about it all night, that's 100 points.

Another thoughtful question. My employer's work is important; it's construction, widely known to many. I approach my duties with dedication, always answer the phone with a smile, and leave customers satisfied. However, there are no queues, and the topic isn't widely discussed. Gratitude is evident in chocolates and champagne, so I'll give myself 25 points.

Question Two: How well-known are you as the best in your field?

If even you are unaware of your talents, and only your family knows you attended school, give yourself 1 point.

If your name is well-known, people ask for your autograph, and meeting you is considered an honor—100 points.

A tricky one. If you want to become wealthy, you'll have to become known—life becomes show business. Right now, only relatives and colleagues know me. My coworkers from other regions share recommendations with me, and I'm considered a good specialist. I'll give myself 11 points.

Question Three: What are you doing to develop your business?

If you do nothing to make your business known, if you avoid people and dream of becoming wealthy in secret, give yourself 1 point.

If you ask yourself daily, "What more can I do to develop my business?", constantly present your work to new people who, in turn, tell others, and your business operates even when you're not there, give yourself 100 points.

That's easier. I have new ideas, meet new people weekly, and somewhat understand development (it's when both money and knowledge grow). Modestly, I'll give myself 6 points.

3. **"D" – DEVELOPMENT:**

- **Work demand – 25 points;**
- **Personal recognition – 11 points;**
- **Business growth – 6 points.**
- Again, we find the average, and we get:

(25 + 11 + 6) / 3 = 14.

- 4. **Fourth Point: -** *Self-Esteem.*
- **First Question: -** *Do you love yourself, do you know yourself, do you know your abilities and talents, do you know your uniqueness and individuality?*
- If you are absolutely certain you're a failure, a nobody, a mistake of nature, boldly write down **1 point.**
- If you know you are perfection, a creation of nature in its celebratory mood; if you know you are incredibly significant for life and thousands of people living on this planet alongside you, write down **10 points.**
- Thoughts of grandeur, a feast in the mind, no thinking required. Of course, I'm great, even good-looking; my mirror in the funhouse told me so. I'm lucky, my tasks succeed, and I know how to connect with people, listen to them, and, most importantly, hear them. Sure, people sometimes call me quirky, but how not to have some fun? Overall, I grew to **8 points.**

- **Second Question: -** *Can you present yourself in such a way that others feel compelled to give you gifts?*
- If people want to run away the moment they see you, and if opening your mouth makes them want to flee for good, write down **1 point.**
- If your presence alone fills people with joy and peace, if your words, gestures, and expressions captivate their attention and make them feel significant; if, after meeting you, people feel better, worthier, happier, and eager to tell others about you, write down **10 points.**
- Hmm, never thought about the speed or direction people might run from me. It seems being a good person isn't enough; you also need to inspire others to be better. I like that idea. How am I now? How do others see me? Nobody seems to complain; their eyes show joy when they see me, and on the phone, they sound glad to hear from me. Of course, there's work to do on myself, but I'd give myself **6 points.**
- **Third Question: -** *Can you sell yourself and your work, and can you show people how much they need your product or service?*
- If you're afraid to even offer your product or ashamed to admit what you do, write down **1 point.**
- If, after meeting you, even Inuit buy snow and desert dwellers buy sand, if people wake up thinking about your product or service, then write down **10 points.**

- No argument here: if you can't sell, you can't get rich. Can I sell? Well, I sold myself to a factory for paper bills with portraits on them. Tried selling on the market once, seemed to go well. Attempted network marketing, nearly lost all my friends. Overall, I'd say **3 points.**
- Again, we find the average value:

$(8 + 6 + 3) / 3 = 5.6$

- 5. **Fifth Point — Ideology.**
- **First Question: -** *Do you have a LIFE GOAL? Are you aware of your MISSION? Do you have a vision of how your LIFE should be arranged for you to feel happy and fulfilled as a person?*
- If you're completely certain your existence is a mistake, if your life goal is to turn yourself into thinking meat with a passport, performing tedious, hateful work on autopilot, and then dying in anger and poverty, write down **1 point.**
- If you are certain that your purpose is TO BE HAPPY, if you are aware of your great talent, if you have a structured plan and clearly envision THE PICTURE OF YOUR LIFE, if you are inspired by what will remain after you, and if you already have a plan for realizing all this, and you're actively working on it every day—bringing new ideas to life weekly—then write yourself **10 points.**
- This one is more intriguing.))) I've discovered my talent, envisioned my life, and even calculated how much it will

cost. Plans are made, I'm investing income into assets. Ideas constantly arise, I'm drafting plans to increase income and dedicate myself to what I love. Altogether, I'd say this deserves *8 points.*

- **Second Question: -** *Do you have a vision of the goals for your business? Do you understand how your business will benefit others? Do you believe that nothing can deter you from your chosen path?*
- *Do you have a vision of how your business is structured, how it operates, who works in it, and what roles they play? Do you have a legend about your business?*
- If you have no idea what needs to be done or have an idea but don't plan to act on it, give yourself *1 point.*
- If you have a legend about your business, if everything is documented and it inspires you, if your legend awakens others and draws them to your cause, if people know what needs to be done and where their role fits in the big picture—if they understand how to start and what the end result will be—then confidently write down *10 points.*
- Another mind-twisting question: A legend about my business? A LEGEND? No, I don't have one.))) But if it's IMPORTANT, I'll create one. I'll draw it, digitize it, organize everything neatly—it's quite enchanting and a must-have. I'll create a beautiful, positive, and successful

story about myself and then bring it to life. For now, I'm learning financial literacy, I have a GOAL, and the cost of that goal is calculated, so I'll give myself *3 points.*

- **Third Question:** *Do you have a team? Are there people inspired by your idea, ready to implement it without you? How PROFESSIONAL is your team, how strong are their characters, and how well do they work together? Can this team generate and execute new ideas, and are they already doing so?*
- If you're alone and haven't decided to act yet, if you're not doing anything even after deciding, give yourself *1 point.*
- If you have a team of friends, if they share your idea passionately, if they co-created a legend about a great endeavor with you, if they act independently and inspire others, if their income formula is maxed out, then write down *10 points.*
- Again, deep in thought. A team, professionals, personalities, strong characters... but I'm alone, completely alone.))) At work, there are colleagues, but not a team. Legends there only exist on TV, and I've never heard dreams from them. It's a collective, not a team: work in the morning, home in the evening. For now, I'll write *1 point; there's room for growth.*
- Let's calculate the average again:

(8 + 3 + 1) / 3 = 4

- Now our task is to combine all these elements into a single formula and find our **INCOME TOTAL.**

  I = P * E * D * S * I

-
  4 * 6.5 * 14 * 5.6 * 4 = **$8,153.**

- So, we see that with this state of affairs, the maximum we can expect is an income of **$8,153.**
- Well, look at that!))) It turns out that by honestly answering these questions, we can precisely determine how much we can earn at maximum if we don't plan to change anything in life. But there's a positive side to this formula: by breaking down these points, we can pinpoint exactly which area needs improvement to increase our income. Here's a hint: fully refining these points to the maximum score will yield a monthly income of **$1,000,000.)))**
- Now, our financial house is fully built, but you've probably noticed it lacks one very important detail. - Correct, *it has no roof.* Now we'll create and firmly secure it!

Protect

The next element of our **"House for Money"** is the roof. What does a roof do? A roof protects, so it must be reliable.

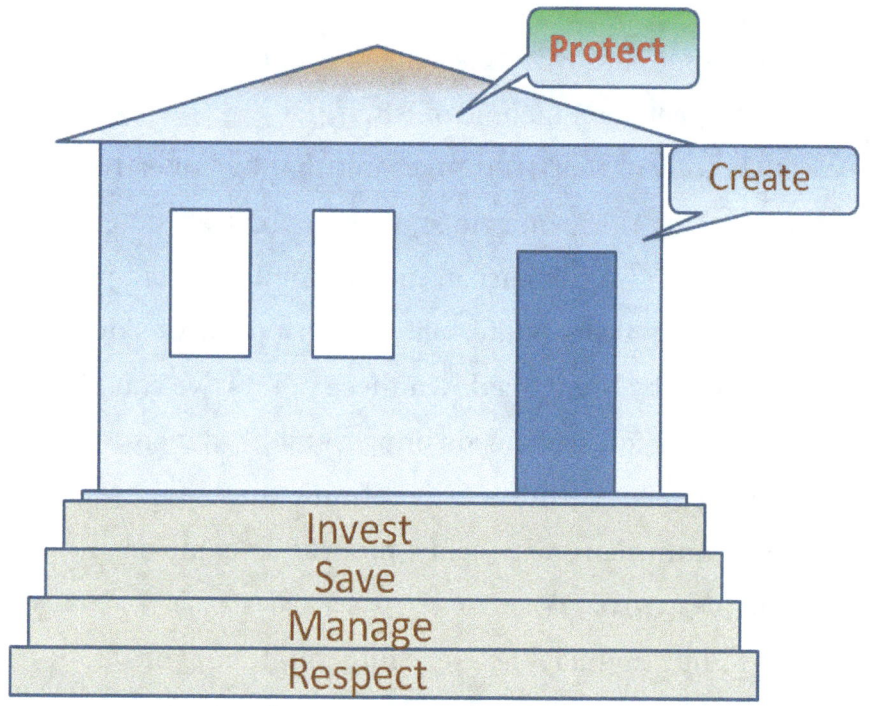

Do you know that as soon as you have money, there are always those eager to take it away? It doesn't have to be thieves, robbers, friends, relatives, sales agents, or tax authorities. What do you think is the main reason we lose money? That's right: when we have no plans, when we ignore what we've learned and spend recklessly, listening to our little dragon "Want-it-all."

If we combine all the reasons for losing money, we identify only three: breaking laws, lack of thoughtful actions, and neglecting basic safety rules. That's why it's important to know three simple protection rules:

PROTECTION STRATEGY

1. **Legality.**
2. **Systematic Approach.**
3. **Safety.**

1. Legality:

This means ensuring your actions comply with the LAW. The laws of unity, for instance: before embarking on something, check whether your actions align with the purpose of others. Does what you plan to do have any useful function for you? Or are you acting without thinking of the consequences? Plan carefully, considering your readiness in terms of money, time, people, and knowledge:

No money: Don't plan or start something requiring money. First, plan how to create funds.

No time for the project: Don't start; plan first how to allocate time.

No people: Plan to find the right people.

No knowledge: Plan to acquire the knowledge you need.

Check your readiness before acting; otherwise, it will be **MUCH MORE EXPENSIVE LATER!**

Legality also pertains to the legality of your business. Your intentions and actions must comply with the laws of the country where you plan to operate. There are many ways to create capital, but among them, seek legal ones and act only within the framework of the LAW. It's crucial to remember: **"WHAT'S ILLEGAL ISN'T PROFITABLE."**

Your accounting may say otherwise, but if you aim to become **FINANCIALLY FREE,** remember that your income streams and capital may attract significant attention from those enforcing the LAW!

BIG MONEY MUST BE LEGAL!

Remember: a freedom capital created outside the law may not lead to freedom but its loss. Keep this in mind.

2. Systematic Approach:

Systematic approach means integrity, using all elements of our HOUSE AS A WHOLE, not just selective parts. Valuing money already protects it because you know its worth.

"The Purchase Act" protects money because it prevents unnecessary spending.

"Savings Program" protects money by preserving what you save.

"Investing" protects money when done wisely and not in overly lucrative scams promising 100% daily returns.)))

"Business System" protects money because it ensures rational investments instead of letting it drift away.

SYSTEMATIC APPROACH MEANS INTEGRITY.

3. Safety:

Safety means responsibility, foresight, and the ability to find answers before questions arise. A highly successful person was once asked how they always managed to make money, even if something didn't go according to plan:

"Because I always have TWO PLANS!"

Plan № 1: How to make money if everything goes according to plan.

Plan № 2: How to make money if nothing goes according to plan.

That's why, no matter what happens, I still make money because I have **Plan #1 and Plan #2.**

Do you see what a safety plan entails? It's the plan developed in collaboration with insurance companies. Remember our kiosk business system? Buy a kiosk and insure it. The kiosk operates, brings joy and profit. If something happens—say, a competitor carelessly tosses a cigarette nearby at night—there's no need for despair because the insurance company compensates you. Because you have **Plan #1 and Plan #2,** you're a responsible person. Before starting anything, check everything, address weak spots, and you'll have peace of mind and protected money.

By developing your ability to protect what you create, you enhance your capability for **FORESIGHT.**

TO PROTECT MEANS TO FORESEE

The next and final element of our **"House for Money"** is **ENJOYMENT.**

Let me ask you: why do we buy a house or an apartment? For the foundation, for the walls, or for the roof? Of course, for the warmth, comfort, safety, and coziness. To live there and enjoy life, for pleasant emotions and states of being.

But the house is just a model, an image, to make it easier to explain how financial freedom is built. A model is easier to understand than just words. And tell me, **WHY DO WE CREATE MONEY?** What is the ultimate **GOAL?**

To survive? — If we don't earn, we can't survive? Is the **PURPOSE OF LIFE TO SURVIVE?**

NO. We create money to **ENJOY.** It is possible to survive without money. **AND IT'S IMPORTANT** not to confuse pleasure and enjoyment. Pleasure is a hook for the will, an urge caught by marketing. You see something in a store and say, "I want it," and there's your "pleasure." But "enjoyment" is a joy of the soul, derived from unity and harmony, from the words "US" and "HARMONIZE." When you and I are in harmony, when there is unity, peace within ourselves and with each other. That feeling of wonder that comes from this unity – that is "Enjoyment."

- Satisfaction is JOY FOR THE MIND, from the words "HOOK" and "CREATE." When the mind creates a hook for someone else's will, it feels satisfaction. Enjoyment is a combination of pleasure, satisfaction, and the delight of unity. It's JOY FOR THE SOUL as a whole. And there is only ONE WAY TO GAIN ENJOYMENT FROM MONEY—TO GIVE IT AWAY TO OTHERS!))) I understand, now's the time to clutch your head and exclaim, "What?"

Yes, the way to gain enjoyment from money is to give it away! And we're discussing this because **THE PURPOSE OF HUMAN LIFE IS TO BE HAPPY!** And happiness is when "WITH PARTS," when all parts of a person receive joy: the

Body, the Mind, and the Soul! When they are in **HARMONY** with one another, then a person experiences **ENJOYMENT.**

But this doesn't mean giving EVERYTHING away! If you give everything, you deny yourself. It's simple: 10% – you invest; this is your money for your future self. 10% – you give to others because this is YOUR MONEY IN OTHER PEOPLE. The rest you spend on yourself, because this is your money FOR YOUR PRESENT SELF.

There's a nuance here I've encountered many times: "When I get rich, I'll definitely help others; it's such a pleasure to help, but only after I'm wealthy." Logically sound, but unfortunately, IT DOESN'T WORK! To help others, you don't have to be rich. After receiving $10, giving away $1 is no big effort. Receiving $100 and giving $10 doesn't choke you either. But imagine you're wealthier now and need to give $100 from $1,000—that's harder. From $10,000—give $1,000? And from $100,000—give $10,000? That becomes practically impossible. So, the promise to "help later" often fails. **YOU NEED TO START WITH SMALL AMOUNTS.** Even here, habits matter. People think the elephant is the mightiest creature, but the frog is stronger; it can sweep away your roof like a feather.

We've clarified that starting small is essential, but here comes another question: why give to others at all? To look like a positive hero in their eyes?

Let's ponder: why is life arranged such that only by giving to others can a person experience **ENJOYMENT?**

Here's the twist: money isn't as much for those who receive it as it is for those who give it. It's not a gift; it's an investment. Other people are also life, so it's an investment in LIFE, and Life always pays back manyfold. The ultimate secret is that LIFE is energy with its own laws, like physics laws, indifferent to hether we know them. Touch the socket, and you'll get shocked.

Money is also energy with its own law, and it will take its 10% no matter what because that's how it works. Life has endless ways to claim its 10%: unpaid debts, failed investments, impulsive purchases... Life will take its due because that's its LAW.
 But knowing this LAW, we can use it. If Life will take its share anyway—GIVE IT WILLINGLY! Anticipate Life—it loves that.)))
Here's the key secret of money:

- Don't give away 10% after receiving money—**GIVE IT IN ADVANCE!**

Think of it as a down payment; you see the product (dream), and to ensure no one else takes it, you make a down payment.
 Want to test yourself? Wondering if you're ready for big money and why you have what you have? Are you ready, right now, to receive $100,000? Truly ready?

- Then right now, take $10,000 (a tithe) from your pocket, find someone in desperate need, and help them immediately! Here's the most IMPORTANT CONDITION! It's simple: - "GIVE IT AWAY AND FORGET." Just enjoy the feeling of what the person you helped experiences—someone who had lost hope. Smile and disappear.

"APPEAR – HELP – DISAPPEAR

THE PURPOSE OF MONEY IS TO SERVE HUMANITY!

www.ingramcontent.com/pod-product-compliance
Lightning Source LLC
Chambersburg PA
CBHW071746240526
45471CB00022B/584